A FIELD GUIDE TO THE
TRACKS AND SIGNS
OF SOUTHERN AND EAST AFRICAN WILDLIFE

A FIELD GUIDE TO THE

TRACKS AND SIGNS

OF SOUTHERN AND EAST AFRICAN WILDLIFE

CHRIS AND TILDE STUART

For Kyle and Leigh, who must still find their trail in life

Struik Nature
(an imprint of Random House Struik (Pty) Ltd)
Reg. No. 1966/003153/07
80 Mckenzie Street, Cape Town, 8001 South Africa
PO Box 1144, Cape Town, 8000 South Africa

Visit us at **www.randomstruik.co.za**
Log on to our photographic website
www.imagesofafrica.co.za for an African experience

First published by Southern Books, 1994; second edition, 1998
Reprinted (third edition) by Struik Publishers, 2000

10 9 8 7

Cover Design by Crazy Cat Design
Illustrations by Tilde Stuart
Set in 10/11 pt Times by 4-Ways DTP Services Cape Town
Production and Design by Wim Reinders & Associates, Cape Town
Reproduction by Unifoto, Cape Town
Printed and Bound by Craft Print International Ltd.

ISBN 978 1 86872 558 8

 # CONTENTS

ACKNOWLEDGEMENTS

The information included in this field guide has been collected over many years and in this process we have come into contact with many individuals who have added to our knowledge. To them all we say thank you very much.

Andre Boshoff, John Carlyon, Penny Meakin, Dave Rowe-Rowe, Roland van Bocxstaele, Harry van Rompaey and Alan Weaving are thanked for filling in our photographic gaps. Penny Meakin drew the caracal skull on page 277. Paul Vercammen and Roland van Bocxstaele are thanked for assistance with information gathering and photographs of the bongo, okapi and African ponguids material.

Louise Grantham of Southern is thanked for her enthusiasm and Marina Pearson for putting a bewildering array of words and illustrations into good order.

1 HOW TO USE THIS BOOK

This book is unique in its approach: instead of listing animals, each with its tracks and signs, in taxonomic order, it allows you to look at the track or signs and then, by means of keys, determine the animal group or species responsible for what you see.

When you see a track you would like to identify, go to the general tracks key on page 14. From there go to the relevant group key, which will direct you to the species description. There you will also find photographs illustrating the tracks under different conditions.

For droppings or dung, go to general droppings key on page 134, which will allow you to determine the group of animals responsible for the droppings. Then read the relevant group description and look at the photographs. If the general droppings key refers you to the antelope, go to antelope dung key on page 138 and check the individual species descriptions and photographs.

To identify bird nests, turn to the key on page 209, which will help you determine to which group your nest belongs.

If you see other signs such as resting places or feeding signs, you will find some guidance as to the identity of the animals responsible in the relevant chapters, but always look for tracks and dung as well.

Tracks differ with living conditions: antelope in sandy areas, for example, may have hoofs longer than usual; tracks in soft sand or mud may be splayed for better purchase.

Always remember that the track of the same species can show considerable variation; this may reflect the age composition of a population (young animals leave smaller tracks), individual differences and the influences of the substrate. For example, a track left in firm, damp silt will usually be clear and will accurately portray the animal's foot structure but if the same individual steps on loose sand the chances of reaching an identification are greatly reduced. This is why it is always a good idea to follow a trail until you find a clear track.

Wherever possible we have included a drawing of the "ideal" track, a photograph of a track taken in the natural state (we have tried to select for what you are most likely to see and not the perfect track) and in some cases the feet themselves where we feel that this may help in reaching a decision on identification. We would like to point out that wherever we have used the feet of animals to illustrate a particular characteristic, none of these animals had been killed specifically to be photographed for this book. Carcasses came from road kills, culling and problem animal control programmes, and predator kills.

Apart from the shape and form of a track, the size is obviously very important. We have given average lengths (without the claws where this is applicable) from hundreds of tracks that we have personally measured and if we consider it important we have included additional measurements, such as greatest width, main pad size and claw length. Wherever possible try to measure tracks that are clear and not distorted.

We have placed the different types of tracks in broad size categories for convenience and where possible similar-sized species occurring in close association are described together. Once you have your track placed in its size group from the comparative plate, turn to the photographs and drawings and take note of the other factors that may aid you in reaching an identification.

2 INTRODUCTION

A vast amount of information can be gleaned about mammals, birds, reptiles and invertebrates without ever having seen them. Although this may sound strange, every animal leaves some indication of its presence or passing, whereby it can be recognised.

Many animals are difficult to observe as they are active during the hours of darkness, or are secretive and spend much of their time under cover. Reading and interpreting animal tracks and signs is a skill that must have been second nature to early humans. Their very survival depended on it, yet only a few hunter-gatherer peoples, such as the San (Bushmen) of the southern deserts and the Pygmies of the equatorial forests, retain this ability. Other than a few hunters and farmers, most people today – including many sport hunters and nature lovers – are unable to tell one track from another or to recognise even obvious signs. And yet, tracking and reading signs can develop into an absorbing pastime in its own right.

It never ceases to amaze us how little many farmers, hunters, professional conservationists and others who spend considerable time in a rural environment know about the activities of the creatures around them. *Homo sapiens* is not the only animal to leave a trail of his passing. Although a particular track or sign may be unfamiliar to you, with some thought and detective work it is often possible to identify the animal that made it and establish what it was doing. It is even possible on occasion to identify a particular individual, such as a leopard with a toe missing – the result of a lucky escape from a gin-trap – or an antelope with a damaged hoof. It is not necessary to see an animal in order to identify it and learn something of its behaviour. The picture you are able to build up about an animal, or species, will often be just as clear and just as accurate as if you had been able to observe the animal. In some cases the picture can be even more reliable.

Almost everywhere you go there are stories to be pieced together from signs. A leopard stalking an impala ewe: the approach tracks, the spot where the predator crouched, the jumping prints with claws extended, the deep tracks left by the antelope in its desperate bid to escape. Blood spots on the sand, a drag mark leading to a dense stand of bush which would have hidden the kill from view and, close by, deep scratch marks gouged into the bark of a tree by the cat after its meal. Most people would walk straight past, totally unaware that an exciting series of events had taken place, but the more observant could piece together a picture quite as fascinating as if the actual kill had been seen. A word of warning: if you are on foot in an area where potentially dangerous game occur (such as lion, leopard, elephant, rhino, hippopotamus, buffalo and Nile crocodile) and you are not "bush-wise," remember the saying, "Fools rush in where angels fear to tread." Better to be a living trainee tracker than a corpse!

Of course, it is a lot easier to read signs in soft ground, but even where the ground is hard and you cannot find tracks, there is usually other evidence of a creature's passing. The stories that can be read are sometimes amusing, sometimes dramatic, but they always lead to a better understanding of the inhabitants of the countryside. We have been collecting information about animals tracks and signs for 15 years, and we can assure you that it is an absorbing pastime.

Where do you start to look for tracks and signs? They are all around you, even in the urban jungle. The "streetwise" pigeon leaves its faecal offerings on windowsills and the bronze heads of past heroes; those globe-trotting rodents, the house mouse and house and brown rats, share our homes and workplaces – you would be surprised! But it is on the farms, in the conservation areas and out there in the "miles and miles of bloody Africa" that you will discover the joys and uses of reading signs, whether you are an urbanite, farmer, conservationist, forester, hunter, hiker or tourist.

The muddy fringes of dams, pans, rain puddles and rivers provide information on the animals that come to drink, feed and wallow, as well as on those that live in, or close to, the water.

Fine silt provides one of the best substrates for locating clear tracks.

Dry riverbeds are found virtually anywhere: they penetrate into even the driest areas. Some streams flow for a limited period each year, others may remain dry for several years. Between floods, sheltered spots may hold surface water, and there is water below the surface in many places, which attract animals that must drink. Many such ephemeral rivers have well developed vegetation along their banks which provides food as well as shade. A number of animals use these riverbeds as "highways" when moving from one area to another.

Man-made gravel and sand roads, as well as paths, are useful sites to look for tracks and signs. Many animals make use of these ribbon-like clearings when on the move: why struggle through long grass and dense bush when there is an easier passage? Such clearings are also used as lying-up areas, for dust-bathing and as hunting grounds. The vegetated fringes provide food for a variety of animals.

Clearings and areas with little vegetative ground-cover may provide good tracking when dry, but during a rain shower old tracks are washed away; a few hours after the thunder-clouds have gone the "clean slate" reveals which creatures have been active since the rain.

Tracks on sand dunes are usually rapidly obliterated by wind, but when tracks are visible dunes provide an excellent tracking locale. Seek out the finer, more compacted sand as tracks will be clearer.

The African coastline is blessed with many, long stretches of open beach. The time between low tide and high tide is the best for seeking tracks as the damp sand retains detail better than the loose sand above the high-water mark.

7

Fence lines, particularly those with wire netting, are often useful tracking locales, as many species burrow under, rather than jump over, these artificial barriers.

Although most signs, particularly tracks, soon disappear there are a few that have survived for millions of years. There are several sites in Africa where you can see the fossilised footprints of dinosaurs and mammal-like reptiles. Most of these tracks had been imprinted in layers of mud, were covered in silt and during the course of time became part of the developing rock, only to be revealed again millennia later by the process of weathering. These tracks were photographed in the vicinity of Mount Etjo in northern Namibia. Droppings of long extinct animals also survive as fossils and provide valuable information on the diet of these prehistoric creatures.

8

The preceding photographs are but a few examples of good places to look for tracks and other signs; remember that there is virtually no site without its animal "notice-boards".

A few pointers to make tracking and sign interpretation easier

☐ Looking is not enough, you have to *see*. Take enough time to study the area around the track or sign that you have found. Merely look and you will not learn, but *see* – pay attention, devote time and effort – and you will understand.

☐ Find out which species occur in the area; read up on their habits – when are they active, are they solitary, do they move in family parties or do they form large herds? A bit of homework goes a long way.

☐ *Never* jump to conclusions. What may seem obvious at first glance could prove to be more complex on closer examination.

☐ Do not walk on the tracks (footprints or spoor) of the animal you are following but walk to the side in case you have to backtrack because you have lost the trail.

☐ *Concentrate* and stay *alert*, always looking for signs to the right and left of you, not just ahead.

☐ Always move *quietly*, as you may be lucky enough to see the animal – always a welcome bonus.

☐ Track *into the sun* wherever possible as this helps to make the track more visible. Tracking is best done when the sun is low, in the early morning and late afternoon. Midday is not good as shadow-casting is poor to non-existent.

☐ Even if you are wearing an expensive pair of designer hiking boots that broke the bank, tear your eyes away and *look several metres ahead* along the trail. You will see more by doing this.

☐ Try to imagine what the animal ahead of you was or is doing: maybe it is heading for water, shelter, or to a feeding site. You will find that with practice amazing accuracy can be achieved.

Measuring, collecting and preserving tracks and other signs

It is always useful to build up a reference collection of track sketches and measurements and there are several ways in which this can be achieved. The sketches that follow show you which measurements are the most important. Include notes on location, habitat and species with each track or sign recorded. Although one can draw tracks on plain paper it is much easier to use graph or blocked paper.

For those who have difficulty making accurate sketches there are two alternatives: tracing or photography. For the former you will need a sheet of perspex (the best size is 30x20 cm) and a waterproof felt-pen. Lay the sheet over the track to be traced but raise it a couple of centimetres above the ground by putting a small stone under each corner. Look directly down onto the track and trace its outline, then take the basic measurements and write them on the sheet. Back at home you can lay tracing paper over the outline on the perspex and copy it, although photocopies can be made directly.

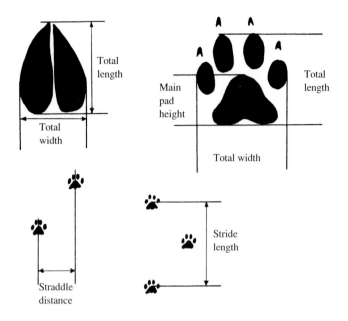

When the copies have been made the sheet can be wiped clean with methylated spirits.

Photography is also a useful tool. It is expensive but one can build up a reference of other signs as well, such as droppings, food remains and shelters. Photographs, like tracings, should be taken from directly above the track. Wherever possible include some form of scale in each photograph. If you use print film the measurements and notes can be written on the back; if slides (transparencies), give each a number and put the information on a small index card.

One can also build up a reference collection of track casts but this takes up plenty of space. For those who are interested in trying this method we give a brief plan of action.

You will need a bottle of water, a mixing bowl or container, a packet of plaster of Paris (quantity depends on the size of the tracks you are casting), a stirring stick and a frame to place around the track to keep the plaster confined. The frame can be a strip of cardboard or thin sheet metal bent in a circle around the track and held in place by a large paper-clip. One can also have several open-ended frames made up but they are bulky and take up much space.

Once you have selected your track, place the frame over it and press it lightly into the substrate. Now estimate how much plaster your "mold" will require. Add a suitable quantity of water to the mixing bowl and slowly add the plaster until it has the consistency of yoghurt or soft porridge. Pour the mixed plaster onto the track to a depth of 2-6 cm, depending on the track size, but do this slowly and carefully or you will ruin the track. You should be patient and leave the plaster to dry for at least 20 minutes before removing the frame. Once the cast is lifted, transport it carefully and leave it to dry thoroughly for 24 hours. You can then brush away loose soil and plant debris. What you now have is a negative of the track. If you wish to make a positive impression, in other words as you saw it in the field, smear the negative impression with vaseline or another non-stick substance, place a frame around the cast (an equivalent height must extend above the original cast) and then pour on the plaster mix. Allow at least 20 minutes for setting and then carefully separate the casts. The positive cast, when dry, can be sprayed or coated with adhesive and sprinkled with fine sand or soil to give it a natural appearance.

For preserving regurgitated bird pellets and mammal droppings you must ensure that they are completely dry. Usually it is sufficient to sun-dry small specimens but it may be necessary to oven-dry larger samples after the initial sun-drying. The dried specimens can be dipped in a commercial, clear sealant which dries rapidly and prevents disintegration. It is advisable to store individual specimens in tubes, bottles or plastic boxes. Each container should be treated with an insecticide (e.g. napthelene crystals) to keep out moths, beetles and mites.

 # 3 TRACKS

One sure sign of an animal's passing is the imprints left by its feet. Not all places, or substrates, will reveal tracks; some will do so only after rain or flooding. Where an animal has walked through dew-soaked grass, or where wind blows across a fine sand surface, some tracks disappear shortly after they are made. On the other hand some tracks may be preserved for long periods in drying mud or in silt; the longest lasting of all are those left by prehistoric creatures (including apemen), which remain as fossils.

In areas of the world where snow falls regularly, animal tracks are relatively easy to locate and identify. In Africa snow, a rarity, is only a feature of certain high mountains and ranges, so we have to rely on other substrates when locating and identifying tracks. Good sites in which to look for tracks include muddy shorelines of lakes, dams and waterholes, the sand and mudbanks along river courses, sandy beaches and dunes (best after light rain or dew), trails and footpaths across fine silt or sand and untarred roadways.

Left and opposite: *Many species make use of trails and it is only rarely possible to view clear sequences of tracks that enable one to determine gaits.*

Tracks (spoor or footprints) may be distinct imprints but very often they are unclear indentations.

An additional aid to species identification from tracks is to examine *gaits*, the position of the footprints in relation to each other. The positioning of some animal tracks is such that one can identify the species by the gait tracks alone. Unfortunately, one does not always have a series of tracks to work from. We have included information on gaits where this may aid you in reaching an identification. The principal gaits are the *walk*, *trot* and *gallop*, and the measurement between the individual tracks is called the *stride*.

When walking, many species place their feet individually so that the tracks do not overlap, but in others the front foot track is covered, or partly covered, by the hind foot track – this is known as registering. In the trot the track positions are similar to those in the walk but the stride is greater. In the gallop the tracks of the four feet are often closely grouped and the stride is at its greatest. In the trot, and particularly in the gallop, the tracks left by the hind feet appear ahead of the imprints of the front feet. A general rule to remember is that the faster the gait, the greater the disturbance of the substrate. However, we must emphasise again that good, clear sequences of tracks over extended distances are rarely found and detailed coverage of this aspect is largely an academic exercise.

GENERAL TRACK KEY

This general key helps you determine the group to which the track belongs that you want to identify. The key refers you to a page or pages with similar tracks, placed at the beginning of each group covered. Here you can identify the animal whose track it is and refer to its species account for further information and illustrations that will enable you to confirm your identification.

PAWS WITHOUT CLAWS
(p 16)

PAWS WITH CLAWS
(p 24)

HANDS AND FEET (p 55)

CLOVEN HOOFS (p 64)

NON-CLOVEN
HOOFS (p 95)

THREE TOES
VISIBLE (p 99)

BIG GAME (p 102)

Hippo

Rhino

Elephant

14

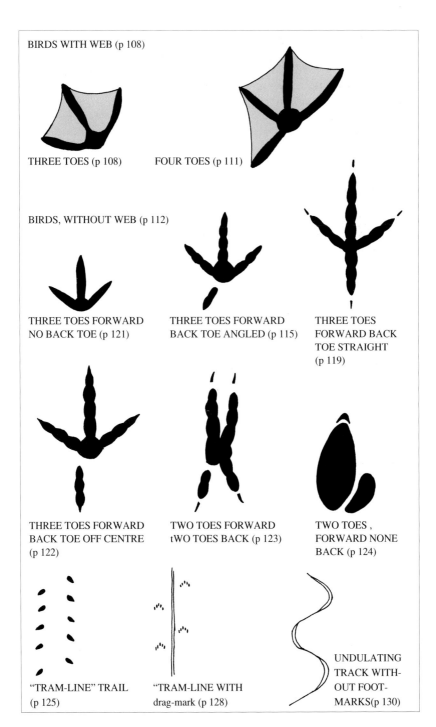

BIRDS WITH WEB (p 108)

THREE TOES (p 108) FOUR TOES (p 111)

BIRDS, WITHOUT WEB (p 112)

THREE TOES FORWARD
NO BACK TOE (p 121)

THREE TOES FORWARD
BACK TOE ANGLED (p 115)

THREE TOES
FORWARD BACK
TOE STRAIGHT
(p 119)

THREE TOES FORWARD
BACK TOE OFF CENTRE
(p 122)

TWO TOES FORWARD
tWO TOES BACK (p 123)

TWO TOES ,
FORWARD NONE
BACK (p 124)

"TRAM-LINE" TRAIL
(p 125)

"TRAM-LINE WITH
drag-mark (p 128)

UNDULATING
TRACK WITH-
OUT FOOT-
MARKS(p 130)

15

PAWS WITHOUT CLAWS

This group includes the cats, with the exception of the cheetah, and the genets. Each foot has a single large pad with two indentations on the posterior edge, which usually but not always show on the track. In the case of the genets these indentations rarely show. Only four toes on each foot come into contact with the ground and they are clearly separated from the main pad. No claw marks are normally visible in the tracks as claws are held in sheaths during normal movement; they are unsheathed only to gain purchase when jumping or for holding down prey. The front feet (pugs) are larger than the hind feet except in the serval and the genets. (The tracks in this key are reproduced in the correct proportion to one another. Measurements refer to specific tracks not averages.)

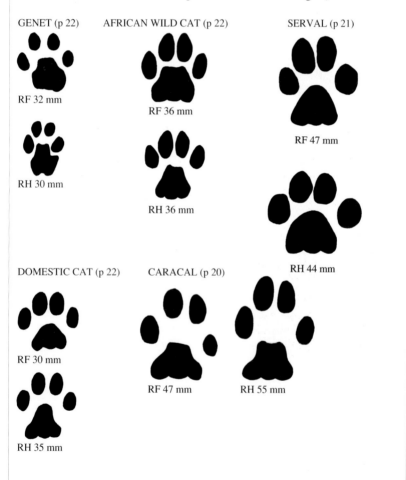

GENET (p 22)

RF 32 mm

RH 30 mm

AFRICAN WILD CAT (p 22)

RF 36 mm

RH 36 mm

SERVAL (p 21)

RF 47 mm

RH 44 mm

DOMESTIC CAT (p 22)

RF 30 mm

RH 35 mm

CARACAL (p 20)

RF 47 mm

RH 55 mm

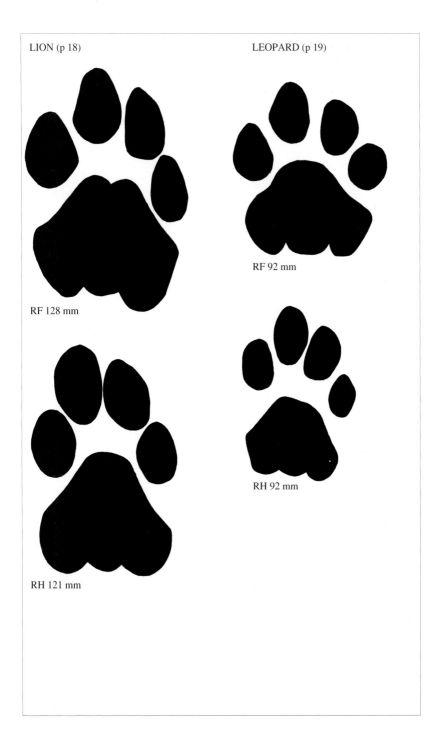

LION (p 18)

LEOPARD (p 19)

RF 92 mm

RF 128 mm

RH 92 mm

RH 121 mm

17

RF

RH

LION

This is the largest African cat and the massive tracks (front 110-130 mm broad and 90-120 mm long; the hind tracks are narrower) are unlikely to be mistaken for those of any other species. Lions usually live in groups (prides) but tracks of lone individuals may be encountered.

Front foot of a lion; note the double indentation on the posterior edge of the main pad and the large toe-pads. The two rounded pads higher up on the leg do not come into contact with the ground.

Clear imprints of lion pugs; the top track is of the hind foot and the lower is of the front foot. Note that the toe-pads of the front foot are more splayed than those of the hind foot.

Lion tracks and human foot imprint; note that the indentations on the posterior edge of the main pad are not visible and the toe pads have spread to gain better purchase on the mud surface. These tracks are of a young lion.

18

RF

RH

LEOPARD

The feet of this large cat are similar to those of the lion but smaller (front track 70-90 mm in length and similar in width; hind track usually 80-100 mm long and 60-80 mm wide). There is considerable geographical variation in the size of leopards, and males are considerably larger than females. The normal walking stride is usually one metre, sometimes more, and the hind foot may be placed on the front foot track. Leopards are solitary animals but females may be accompanied by one to three cubs.

Clear front track of a leopard; note its rounded appearance and the double indentation on the posterior edge of the main pad.

Front (above) and hind tracks of a leopard; note that the double indentations are not visible.

The front foot of an adult leopard; note the cracks on the main pad – in fine soils these could be visible and allow for individual identification.

RF

RH

CARACAL

Caracal tracks are similar in shape and form to those of the leopard but smaller (front tracks are rounded and usually 50-55 mm long and equally wide; hind tracks average 45-50 mm in length and 42-48 mm in width). The normal walking stride is about 60-80 cm. The hind foot is usually placed partly over the track left by the front foot. Usually a solitary animal.

Front foot of a caracal; the double indentation on the posterior edge of the main pad and the overall rounded appearance is typical of all cats.

The hind foot of the caracal is narrower than the front foot.

Although during normal locomotion the cats keep the claws sheathed, they may leave visible claw marks when leaping at prey. Here a caracal had leaped at, and caught, a scrub hare: note the clear marks left in the sand by the claws and the double indentation on the posterior edge of the main pad of the top track.

RF

RH

SERVAL

Serval tracks are similar to those of the caracal but somewhat smaller (40-50 mm in length) and the hind print is more rounded. This species is a solitary wanderer, although pairs are not uncommonly observed.

Note that the indentations on the posterior edge of the main pad are not as well developed as in the other cat species.

Serval tracks in lightly wind-blown sand; the hind foot track is at the top. Note the impala track bottom right.

AFRICAN WILD CAT and DOMESTIC CAT

The tracks left by the African wild cat and its domestic cousin are identical in appearance but those of the former are slightly larger (length of front and hind tracks averages 30-35 mm) and in both cases the hind track is slightly narrower than the front track. The normal walking stride is about 30 cm, increasing to 40 cm or more when the cat is trotting. These cats are predominantly solitary creatures. In the drier areas of southern Africa you may encounter tracks of the rare small-spotted cat, but these tracks rarely exceed a length of 22 mm (see the genets).

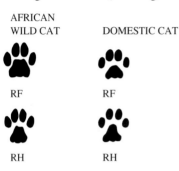

AFRICAN
WILD CAT   DOMESTIC CAT

RF   RF

RH   RH

The front foot of an African wild cat with claws unsheathed. The toe-pads are usually quite splayed when the cat is walking, particularly those of the front feet. Note the typical double indentation on the posterior edge of the main pad.

RF

RH

GENETS

It is not possible to identify the different genet species on tracks alone. Although each foot has five toes, only four show in the tracks; the claws are retracted; the main pad has two indentations like those of the cats but these rarely show clearly on the track. The tracks are smaller than those of the African wild cat (20-22 mm long and 22-24 mm wide). The tracks left by the front feet are slightly larger than those left by the hind feet. Genets are solitary species. Despite the track similarities these animals are not members of the cat family.

The front foot of a small-spotted genet; note the cat-like appearance.

The hind foot of a small-spotted genet; only the main pad and toe-pads come into contact with the ground.

The front foot track of a genet in dried silt; note the powdered silt that has blown into the track.

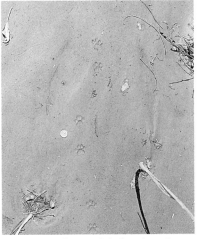

A genet walking trail showing clearly the similarity between front and hind tracks. The large size of the main pad and the proximity of the toe-pads to the main pad can be clearly seen.

23

PAWS WITH CLAWS

This large group includes the dogs, jackals, foxes, hyaenas, mongooses and civets, the cheetah, spotted-necked otter, honey badger, striped polecat and striped (white-naped) weasel, the shrews, elephant shrews, hedgehogs, hares and rabbits, and the rodents. They have one thing in common: the tracks of all these species show claw marks to a lesser or greater degree. Although many of the species have five toes on each foot, in a number of cases only four toe-pad impressions are visible. We have grouped similar looking tracks together, even where species do not belong to the same family, for ease of identification. The tracks are also placed in similar size groupings, which should further aid you in determining the identity of the species. *Please note* that measurements given for these tracks exclude the claws, because their length varies considerably among species.

PAWS WITH CLAWS – LARGE
(measurements without claws)

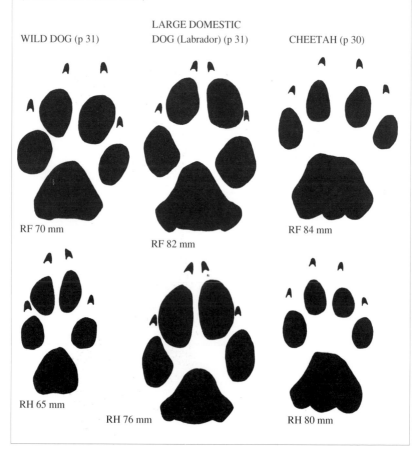

WILD DOG (p 31)

LARGE DOMESTIC
DOG (Labrador) (p 31)

CHEETAH (p 30)

RF 70 mm

RF 82 mm

RF 84 mm

RH 65 mm

RH 76 mm

RH 80 mm

24

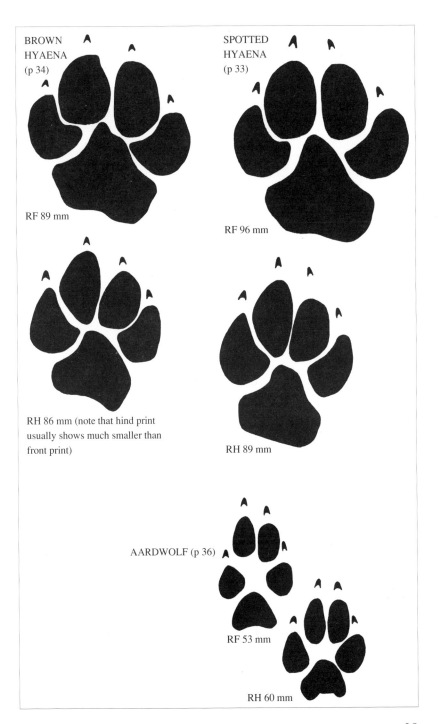

BROWN
HYAENA
(p 34)

RF 89 mm

RH 86 mm (note that hind print
usually shows much smaller than
front print)

SPOTTED
HYAENA
(p 33)

RF 96 mm

RH 89 mm

AARDWOLF (p 36)

RF 53 mm

RH 60 mm

PAWS WITH CLAWS – MEDIUM TO LARGE

(measurements without claws)

AFRICAN CIVET (p 40)　　SPOTTED-NECKED OTTER (p 40)　　PORCUPINE (p 38)

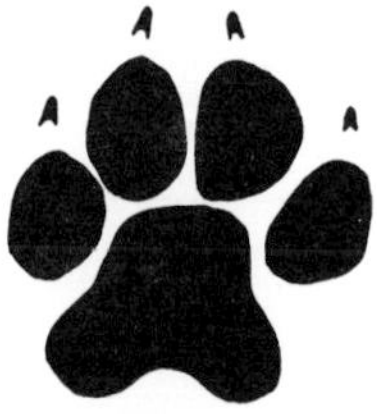

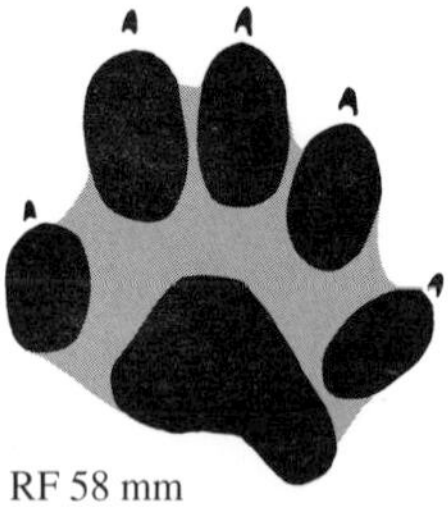

RF 45 mm　　　　　RF 58 mm　　　　　　　RF 50 mm

RH 52 mm

RH 70 mm

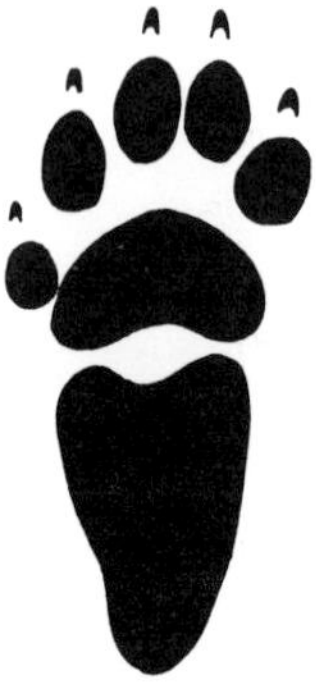

RH 81 mm

HONEY BADGER
(RATEL) (p 37)

RF 54 mm

RH 81 mm

PAWS WITH CLAWS – MEDIUM

(measurements without claws)

BAT-EARED FOX
(p 42)

RF 39 mm

RH 36 mm

CAPE FOX
(p 43)

RF 40 mm

RH 36 mm

SMALL DOMESTIC DOG
(p 44)

RF 41 mm

RH 43 mm

BLACK-BACKED JACKAL
(p 41)

RF 51 mm

RH 56 mm

SIDE-STRIPED JACKAL
(p 42)

RF 43 mm

RH 47 mm

PAWS WITH CLAWS – MEDIUM TO SMALL

(measurements without claws)

LARGE GREY
MONGOOSE (p 45)

RF 42 mm

RH 44 mm

WHITE-TAILED
MONGOOSE (p 46)

RF 41 mm

RH 41 mm

WATER
MONGOOSE (p 46)

RF 41 mm

RH 36 mm

YELLOW
MONGOOSE (p47)

RF 25 mm

RH 25 mm

BANDED
MONGOOSE (p 48)

RF 29 mm

RH 29 mm

DWARF
MONGOOSE (p 49)

RF 16 mm

RH 16 mm

SMALL GREY
MONGOOSE (p 49)

RF 25 mm

RH 28 mm

SLENDER
MONGOOSE (p 50)

RF 23 mm

RH 25 mm

SURICATE (p 48)   STRIPED WEASEL (p 50)   STRIPED POLECAT (p 50)

RF 20 mm   RF 21 mm   RF 22 mm

RH 23 mm   RH 15 mm   RH 22 mm

PAWS WITH CLAWS – VERY SMALL
(measurements without claws)

GIANT RAT (p 52)	SOUTHERN GROUND SQUIRREL (p 52)	TREE SQUIRREL (p 52)	SHREW (p 53)	SOUTHERN AFRICAN HEDGEHOG (p 53)
RF 24 mm	RF 30 mm	RF 25 mm	RF 7 mm	RF 18 mm
RH 32 mm	RH 45 mm	RH 46 mm	RH 15 mm	RH 22 mm

ROUNDEARED ELEPHANT SHREW (p 53)   RF 7 mm

RH 16 mm

STRIPED MOUSE (p 54)   RF 10 mm

RH 14 mm

PAWS WITH CLAWS – LARGE

Here we include the large domestic dog, the hyaenas (also the aardwolf), the wild dog and the cheetah.

RF

RH

CHEETAH

The cheetah has a typical cat foot structure, with the double indentation on the posterior edge of the main pad, but claw marks are usually visible on the track. Tracks could be confused with those of the wild dog but can be told by the different main pad impression: that of the dog is roughly triangular and lacks the indentations. The tracks are more elongated and smaller than those of either lion or leopard (front foot averages 85 mm in length and 75 mm in width, hind foot slightly longer but fractionally narrower). Cheetah are either solitary or live in small groups of two to five individuals.

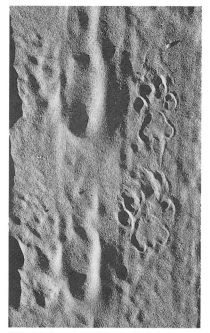

Hind (above) and front (below) tracks of a cheetah; claw marks are hardly visible.

The hind foot imprint of a cheetah, with claw marks visible.

30

RF

WILD DOG

Wild dog tracks are similar to those of a large domestic dog, with roughly triangular main pads and four toe imprints left by each foot. The claws are blunt and thick and show clearly on the track. Front tracks are broader than hind tracks but the latter are marginally longer (front track 76-80 mm long and 56-65 mm wide; hind track 68-82 mm long and 48-55 mm wide). We emphasise again that all the measurements we give should be seen as guidelines and not as rules. This animal runs in packs. Compare the tracks with those of the hyaenas.

RH

Front and hind tracks of a wild dog; note the roughly triangular main pad impressions and the marks left by the heavy claws.

RF

LARGE DOMESTIC DOG

Domestic and feral dogs may be encountered not only near human habitation but also away from it. Large dog tracks could be confused with those of the cheetah (which however have indentations on the main pad), the hyaenas (massive structure and angled main pad) and the wild dog (rarity). The main pad is roughly triangular with a pointed anterior edge, the toe-pads are large and in close contact with the main pad, and blunt claw marks are always present. Members of the dog family have a more or less straight posterior edge to the main pad. See also

RH

the section on the small dog. Sizes are not given as they vary considerably with the different breeds.

Front foot of a large dog; note the roughly triangular main pad and the large, rounded toe-pads.

Hind foot of a large dog; the toe-pads may be more elongated than those of the front foot. Note the heavy, blunt claws.

Track of a large dog's front foot in thin mud. Note the close proximity of the toe-pads to the main pad, the distinct claw marks and the straight posterior edge of the main pad impression.

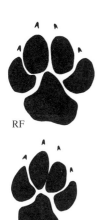

RF

RH

SPOTTED HYAENA

This is the largest of the three hyaena species and is found widely in sub-Saharan Africa. All species have front feet larger than the hind feet but this seems to be less marked in the spotted hyaena. The average length of the front foot is 96 mm and the hind foot 89 mm; however, we have measured front tracks of almost 106 mm. The main pad is large and its posterior edge angled; the massive toe-pads lie in close proximity to the main pad. The claws are blunt and leave substantial imprints.

The front (above) and hind tracks of a spotted hyaena.

Spotted hyaena tracks crossing from left to right (hind is the smaller), with lion tracks for comparison at right.

RF

RH

BROWN HYAENA

The brown hyaena is restricted to southern Africa. Tracks, mostly of solitary individuals, are most commonly encountered along the coast of Namibia and in the Kalahari. Tracks are similar to those of the spotted hyaena but the hind track is noticeably smaller. The average front track length is 85 mm but the hind track is only 66 mm.

Brown hyaena tracks; the larger track is left by the front foot. Note the angled hind pad and the massive toe-pads.

In fine silt or sand the hair on the upper part of the foot may leave marks around the track. This is not observed in the other two hyaena species. Note the large size of the front track (the lowest track in the photograph).

Striped hyaena tracks. Note also the Grevy's zebra and beisa oryx tracks; it is always useful to have the tracks of several species together for comparison.

RF

RH

AARDWOLF

The feet of the aardwolf are considerably smaller than those of the true hyaenas. Front track length is 44 mm, hind length 42 mm. Remember that these measurements exclude the length of the claws, which in this species could add 10-15 mm to the overall length. The main pads are relatively small and are roughly triangular, as is the case with members of the dog family. The toe-pads are large and the claws are well developed, particularly those of the front feet, which are used for digging.

The front foot of the aardwolf is larger than the hind foot and the claws are more robust.

The narrower hind foot of the aardwolf.

A particularly large front foot imprint of an aardwolf; the size is slightly exaggerated because the animal was walking on wet mud and the toe-pads were widely splayed.

PAWS WITH CLAWS – MEDIUM TO LARGE
In this group we have placed the honey badger, porcupine, African civet and spotted-necked otter.

RF

RH

HONEY BADGER (RATEL)
This stocky, medium-sized carnivore has large feet for its size; the front feet are equipped with long (up to 25 mm), powerful claws for digging. The front foot tracks average 80 mm in length and those of the hind foot 65 mm. Although the pad behind the main pad (called the proximal pad) on all feet may show, in our experience it is often indistinct, particularly on the track of the front foot. The proximal pad may add an additional 20 mm to the overall length. Each foot has five toes but in many cases only four show clearly in the track. This is largely dependent on the substrate. The honey badger is a loner and may be encountered in most habitats.

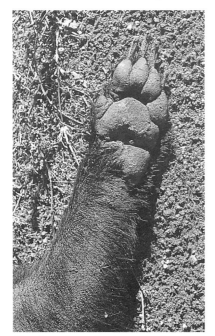

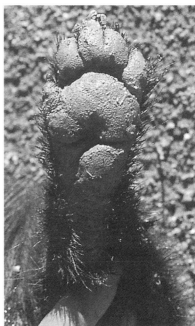

The front foot of a honey badger; note the substantial pads and the well developed claws for digging. The proximal pad may or may not show in the track.

The claws of the hind feet are much shorter.

37

Front foot track of a honey badger; note the distance that the claw marks lie from the toe-pads.

The hind foot track could be mistaken for that of a porcupine but if you locate the front track the marks left by the long claws will confirm your identification.

RF

RH

PORCUPINE

This is the largest African rodent. The tracks could be confused with those left by the honey badger. The front track averages 70 mm in length and the hind track about 80 mm. Although there are five toes on each foot, only four are seen on the front foot tracks. The claws of the front feet are robust but they are much shorter than those of the honey badger. The porcupine is usually a solitary forager but trails may be used by several animals. Always watch out for the black-and-white banded quills that are dropped along regularly used porcupine trails.

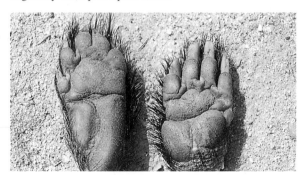

Hind foot and front foot of a porcupine. Note the heavy but short claws on the front foot.

Front (above) and hind tracks of a porcupine in coarse sand.

Porcupine tracks (in centre) in fine river silt showing all pad details; this is a rare find. Note also the horse tracks on the left and the narrower donkey tracks to the right. There are also the three-toed tracks of a dikkop in the lower part of the photograph.

This photograph was taken further along the trail shown in the previous picture. Although the footprints of the porcupine are indistinct at this point, the scratch marks left by the lower rump quills are clearly visible. About five metres further we were able to pick up the footprints again.

RF

RH

SPOTTED-NECKED OTTER

Of the three otter species occurring in sub-Saharan Africa, only this species has true webbing between the toes and claws on the feet. There are five toes on each foot; these usually show in the track but the webbing and claws are not always clear. Hind track length is some 60-70 mm and front track length 60-65 mm. This species is widespread but rarely found away from suitable water bodies.

RF

RH

AFRICAN CIVET

The tracks of this species could be confused with those of a small dog (front track 50 mm long and 55 mm wide; hind track 48 mm by 42 mm), but the posterior edge of the main pad is slightly concave. Toe-pads are large and located close to the anterior edge of the main pad. The claw marks are blunt and close to the toe-pad tracks. Although this is a solitary species you may encounter the tracks of several individuals at latrine sites.

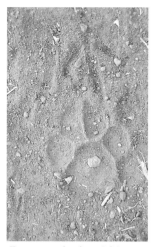

Front track of an African civet.

Hind track of an African civet.

Walking track of an African civet.

In this group we have included the jackals, foxes and the small domestic dog. They all have roughly triangular main pads; four toes and distinct claw marks show in each track. The tracks of the black-backed, common (golden) and side-striped jackals are very similar and difficult to separate.

RF

RH

BLACK-BACKED JACKAL

This, the most widespread jackal in southern Africa, is also common in parts of east Africa. The front track averages 54 mm in length and 40 mm in width; the hind track is noticeably smaller, 43 mm by 32 mm. Although the black-backed jackal is usually a solitary hunter, it is not unusual to encounter pairs and small groups.

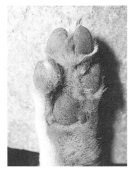

Far left: *The front foot of a black-backed jackal; note the large, triangular main pad. The two middle toes extend well beyond the outer toes.*
Left: *The hind foot; the main pad is smaller than that of the front foot but the two middle toes also extend forward.*

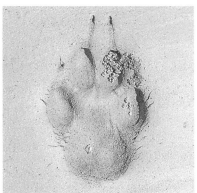

The front track of a black-backed jackal; the claws are usually longer in animals that live in sandy areas.

The walking trail of a black-backed jackal.

RF

 RH

SIDE-STRIPED JACKAL
The tracks are difficult to separate from those of the previous species.

 RF

RH

BAT-EARED FOX
The tracks of this fox are much smaller than those of the jackals (front 35 mm, but the claws may extend a further 18 mm; hind 32 mm and narrower than the front track). The claws of the middle two toes of the front foot are close together in the track. The pad impressions of the hind foot are often obscured by the long hair. This animal is usually seen in small parties of three to six.

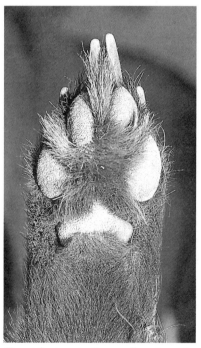

Front foot; note the small main pad and the long claws on the two middle toes.

Hind foot shows the dense hair covering that may obscure the pad prints. The claws are shorter than those on the front feet.

RF

RH

CAPE FOX

This fox is found only in southern Africa. There is pronounced hair growth between the foot-pads and this may obscure the tracks, particularly in sand. The average front track length is 38 mm, the hind track is slightly shorter. As in the bat-eared fox the two middle toes on each foot are close together and extend well forward of the outer toes, giving the tracks a pointed appearance.

The front foot of a Cape fox; note the dense hair covering and the closeness of the middle toes.

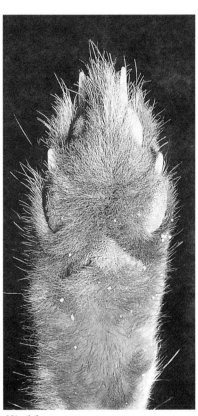

Hind foot.

SMALL DOMESTIC DOG

RF   RH

The track of a terrier; note the stout, triangular main pad and the large toe-pad impressions that lie close to the anterior edge of the main pad. The claw marks are short but stout.

The running track of a small domestic dog.

PAWS WITH CLAWS – MEDIUM TO SMALL

All mongooses fall within this group, as well as the striped polecat and the striped weasel. We have only included the tracks of the abundant mongooses as many species are rare or localised, or their signs are rarely encountered. It is very difficult to separate the species on tracks alone. Although most mongooses have five toes on each foot, it is common to see only four toe marks in each track. The main pad is well developed and the toe-pads are clearly separated from it. There are distinct claw marks with each track.

This group of tracks also includes those of the hares and rabbits, squirrels, giant rat and hedgehogs. We concede that these are generally difficult to separate to species level but by looking at distribution and habitat preference you should be able narrow down your choice. Take into account which species are solitary and which ones forage in troops, which are closely associated with water and which ones inhabit arid areas. As always when interpreting tracks and signs, never rely on only one line of investigation; examine the broader picture.

LARGE GREY MONGOOSE

The front track averages 42 mm in length and has a width of 35 mm, the hind track being only slightly smaller. This species frequents areas close to water. Although it is mainly solitary, small numbers may move together.

RF

RH

Walking trail of a large grey mongoose.

RF

RH

WHITE-TAILED MONGOOSE

The tracks of front and hind feet are the same size (front track averages 45 mm in length) and could be mistaken for those of a jackal but the toe-pad impressions are smaller. This solitary species is widespread in the tropics and frequents a wide range of savanna habitats.

White-tailed mongoose tracks.

RF

RH

WATER MONGOOSE

The tracks of this mongoose are commonly found in riverside mud and on the fringes of other water bodies throughout sub-Saharan Africa. Five toe-pad prints may be visible in each track but the inner toe mark is often indistinct. The toes are long and slender and the track is superficially bird-like, but the presence of at least four forward-pointing toe tracks is distinctive. Front track length averages 46 mm, and the hind foot track is usually slightly longer. During normal walking the hind foot is commonly placed over the track of the front foot. This is a solitary animal but in favoured areas tracks may be abundant.

Part of the walking trail of a water mongoose. It could be confused with that of the Nile monitor (water leguaan) but that reptile leaves a tail drag mark between the footprints.

Water mongoose tracks (four forward-pointing toes) leading from right to left and those of a crow (three forward-pointing toes) leading from left to right.

RF

RH

YELLOW MONGOOSE

This small, diurnal mongoose lives in small colonies but is a solitary forager. The tracks resemble those of the small grey mongoose, which has the same distribution, but the species can usually be separated on habitat preferences: the yellow mongoose lives in more open country. The front track averages 26 mm in length and the hind track is noticeably narrower.

RF

RH

SURICATE

The suricate and the previous species occur in similar habitats in the western parts of southern Africa and may even share the same warrens. Suricate tracks are similar to those of the yellow mongoose (average length is 24-26 mm) but the claws of the front feet are much longer (reaching 15 mm) and their imprints usually show clearly in the track. Suricates live in colonies of five to as many as 40 individuals. The tracks are usually found in association with numerous small, conical holes where the animals have dug for insects.

Note the impressions made by the long claws.

RF

RH

BANDED MONGOOSE

The banded mongoose, also a colonial species, is widespread in sub-Saharan Africa. Because these animals live in troops you are not likely to encounter the tracks of a solitary banded mongoose. If you identify a solitary track as that of a banded mongoose you've made a mistake: try again! Although only four toes show clearly on the front foot track, a small fifth toe may show up in soft soil. The front track averages 26 mm in length.

Front (above) and hind tracks of a banded mongoose. The fifth, inner toe has left a slight impression on the front track.

RF

RH

DWARF MONGOOSE

The tracks have no outstanding features, except for their small size (length averages 16 mm); the claw marks may lie 8 mm ahead of the front track. This colonial species lives in savanna areas.

RF

RH

SMALL GREY MONGOOSE

A common, solitary mongoose in southern and western areas of southern Africa. The front track averages 28 mm in length and the hind track is only slightly smaller.

Front foot of the small grey mongoose; note the small inner toe, which rarely leaves a clear impression in the track.

The hind foot; the small inner toe rarely shows in the track.

Tracks of a small grey mongoose.

Walking trail of a small grey mongoose; note how the hind foot tracks have registered over the front tracks.

SLENDER MONGOOSE
A solitary and very widespread species. The tracks are similar to those of the previous species but 2-3 mm shorter, the claw marks are finer and the toe-pad impressions usually not as bold.

STRIPED POLECAT
The track of this lone wanderer is characterised by five clear toe impressions and claw marks some 10 mm from the pads on the front tracks. Front tracks range from 20-28 mm in length and those of the hind foot 20-26 mm. The normal walking stride is approximately 15 cm. Tracks resemble those of the honey badger but are much smaller.

STRIPED (WHITE-NAPED) WEASEL
Striped weasel tracks are similar to those of the dwarf mongoose but this species is a strict loner and its tracks are seldom found and easily overlooked. Front tracks are about 18 mm long and those of the hind foot 15 mm, and the claw marks are close to the toe-pads.

HARES and RABBITS

The undersides of the feet of the hares and rabbits are characterised by a thick layer of strong, springy hairs that leave indistinct print impressions. The claw marks, particularly the five on the front tracks, usually show. The best identification pointer is not the individual footprint but the positioning of the feet. The hind feet come to rest close together, with the front feet tracks more or less one behind the other, but to the rear of the hind footprints. Members of this group are very widely distributed.

Front foot of a scrub hare, showing the springy mat of hair and the claws.

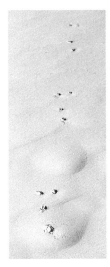

Typical set of hare tracks; the hind foot impressions lie paired and ahead of the front foot tracks. Note the claw marks.

A hare or rabbit sits on the full length of the hind feet but when it is on the move only the front of the hind feet comes into contact with the ground.

PAWS WITH CLAWS – VERY SMALL

In most cases it is not possible to identify animals of this group to species level without taking into account such aspects as distribution and habitat preference.

RF

RH

GROUND SQUIRRELS

Several species of ground squirrel occur in the savanna and semi-arid areas of Africa but tracks are similar in all cases. The front foot track of the southern ground squirrel averages 22 mm in length and the hind track 60 mm, but the entire length of the hind foot does not always come into contact with the ground. The claw marks (four in front; five behind) are always clear.

The hind foot normally steps on the track made by the front foot. In the centre of the photograph you can see where the squirrel has sat: the impressions left by the bushy tail are very clear.

RF

RH

TREE SQUIRRELS

As their name implies these rodents spend much of their time in trees and bushes but some species do forage on the ground. The tracks are very similar to those of the ground squirrels but the groups can usually be clearly separated by their habitat preferences. The full length of the hind foot usually makes an impression only when the animal is sitting.

RF

RH

GIANT RAT

As its name implies, this is a large rodent (up to 3 kg). It lives in forests and dense woodland in the tropics. The front track is about 20 mm in length; if the entire hind foot comes into contact with the soil it leaves a track of about 50 mm but when the rat is walking only the front section may leave an impression. The tracks could be mistaken for those of the large tree squirrels.

RF

RH

HEDGEHOGS
There are two common hedgehog species, one occurring in southern and the other in east Africa. The southern species has five toes but the northern only four. The tracks left by front and hind feet average 26 mm in length. The most important identification factor is the wide straddle (30-60 mm). The hind foot tracks may or may not register in those of the front.

Tracks of the southern African hedgehog; note the straddle and the hind tracks registered in those of the front. When walking slowly hedgehogs may drag the hind feet.

RF

RH

SHREWS
Well over 150 species of shrew are known from sub-Saharan Africa. Most species have a mass of only a few grams and therefore tracks are rarely found. Shrews walk on the full length of the feet (plantigrade); each foot has five toes and each has a claw. Track length varies from species to species but the forest shrew has a front foot length of 7 mm and hind 9 mm. The tail may leave a drag mark between the footprints. The only place where we have ever found clear shrew tracks is in fine, damp river silt.

RF

RH

ELEPHANT SHREWS
Several species live in rocky habitats and their tracks are seldom found but others occupy areas where tracks may be located. Locomotion is usually in a series of hops and regularly used trails may show as a series of small oval patches of bare ground interspersed with undisturbed debris and vegetation.

53

RF

RH

SMALL MICE

Here we have only distinguished between the hopping locomotion of many of the gerbil species and the tracks of the
"ordinary" mice.

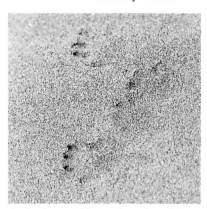

*A single set of hairy-footed gerbil
tracks; note that the more widely
separated tracks are made by the
hind feet. Claw marks may be visible
but this depends on the substrate.*

Top: *Gerbil tracks descending in
soft sand. Note the beetle track at
upper centre.*

Left: *The tracks in the lower part of
the photograph were made by a
striped mouse and the upper tracks
by a hairy-footed gerbil.*

*Three sets of gerbil tracks in hard,
medium-hard and soft sand.*

HANDS AND FEET

All the primates (monkeys and apes), the clawless otters and the hyraxes (dassies) fall into this group. In all cases the nails are short and may or may not show in the track.

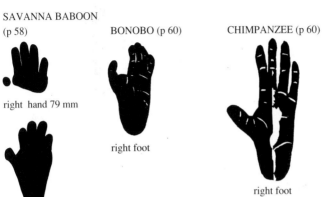

SAVANNA BABOON
(p 58)

right hand 79 mm

right foot 137 mm

BONOBO (p 60)

right foot

CHIMPANZEE (p 60)

right foot

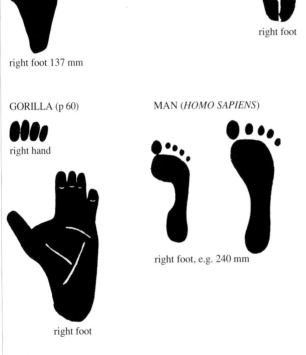

GORILLA (p 60)

right hand

right foot

MAN (*HOMO SAPIENS*)

right foot, e.g. 240 mm

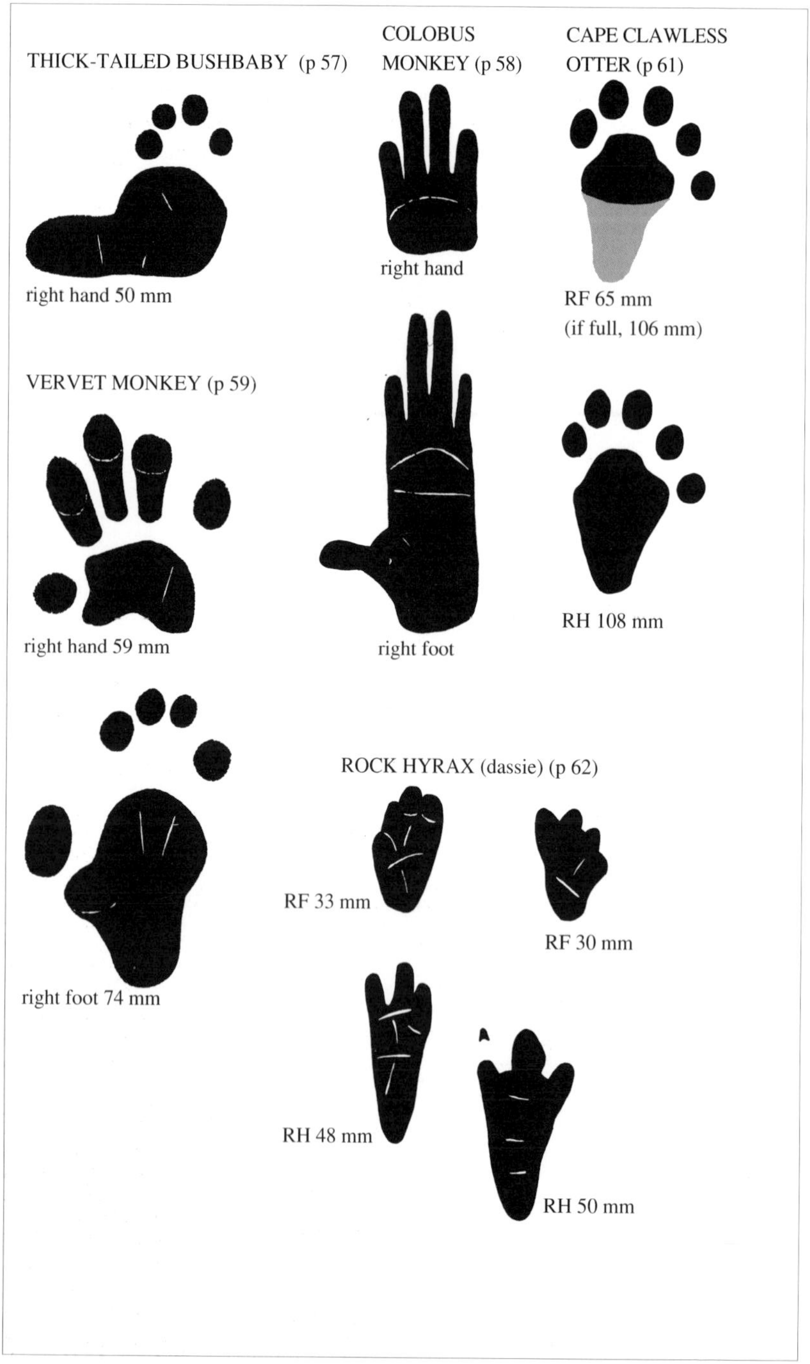

THICK-TAILED BUSHBABY (p 57)

right hand 50 mm

COLOBUS MONKEY (p 58)

right hand

CAPE CLAWLESS OTTER (p 61)

RF 65 mm
(if full, 106 mm)

VERVET MONKEY (p 59)

right hand 59 mm

right foot

RH 108 mm

right foot 74 mm

ROCK HYRAX (dassie) (p 62)

RF 33 mm

RF 30 mm

RH 48 mm

RH 50 mm

Right hand

THICK-TAILED BUSHBABY

In our experience this is the bushbaby species that most frequently moves around on the ground. It occurs widely in the eastern parts of southern Africa and in east Africa. The tracks show the marks of the very large thumb and big toe, with both standing at right angles to the hands and feet. The front foot is about 50 mm in length and the hind foot may reach almost 100 mm.

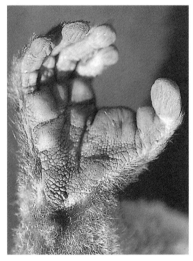

The hand of a thick-tailed bushbaby showing the massively developed thumb.

The hand track of this bushbaby; note the small impressions left by the four fingertips.

Tracks of several bushbabies in the vicinity of a waterhole.

Right hand

Right foot

BABOONS

The baboons, of which there are several species, are large primates that spend most of their foraging time on the ground, where they leave distinctive tracks. They live in troops, predominantly in savanna country.

The foot of a savanna baboon; in the track the big toe usually stands out from the foot at an angle of about 45°. The average track length is 140 mm.

Hand of the same animal; only the area forward of the thumb comes into contact with the ground and the thumb usually stands out at a 75° angle.

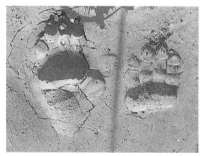

Foot and hand print of a baboon in river silt.

The walking trail of a baboon in fine sand.

58

Right hand

Right foot

VERVET MONKEY

The vervet monkey leaves tracks typical of the guenons (true monkeys), and we include material on only this species. This monkey occurs widely in African woodland savannas. It is more terrestrial than most other species and the tracks are commonly found.

The tracks are similar to those of the baboons but smaller (front 55 mm; hind 85 mm).

Tracks of vervet monkeys in fine sand; note where the animals sat down and left imprints of their tails.

Right hand

Right foot

COLOBUS MONKEY

All the colobus monkeys occur in the forests of tropical Africa and only occasionally forage on the ground. The fingers and toes are long and thin and there are no thumbs on the hands.

Right hand

Right foot

GORILLA

This, the largest of all the primates, is restricted to the tropical and montane forests close to the Equator. The footprints are longer and broader than those of the human foot, and the large big toe stands at an angle away from the foot. This species uses only the knuckles of the hand when walking, leaving four oval impressions in the soil.

Knuckle impressions left by the hand of a gorilla (Photo: Harry van Rompaey).

Foot imprint of an eastern lowland gorilla (Photo: Roland van Bocxstaele).

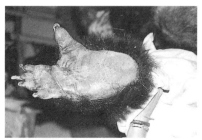

Underside of the foot of an adult male eastern lowland gorillla. The lenght of the nails in wild living gorillas is much shorter. (Photo: Roland van Bocxstaele).

Knuckle imprint of an eastern low-land gorilla (Photo: Roland van Bocxstaele).

CHIMPANZEE AND BONOBO

These species have similar tracks but their distributions do not overlap. Both the hands and the feet are long but smaller and more slender than those of the gorilla. Like their larger cousin these animals also use only the knuckles of the hands when walking.

CHIMPANZEE

right foot

BONOBO

right foot

CLAWLESS OTTERS

There are two species of clawless otter, the Congo and Cape, but the latter has by far the greater distribution. Although the feet measure 145 mm and the hands 100 mm, the tracks do not always show their full length (foot tracks are 100 mm; hand 70 mm). If the animal had been walking in soft sand or mud, the tracks may appear in full length but in harder substrates only the imprints of the toes and fingers and the anterior edge of the main pad may show.

RF

RH

Note the primate-like fingers of the Cape clawless otter.

A single clawless otter track in mud; note the absence of claw marks.

The walking trail of a clawless otter.

Back foot track of a Cape clawless otter.

ROCK

RF RF

RH RH

HYRAXES (DASSIES)

There are several species of hyrax and they are abundant in some areas. Because of their rocky and forested habitats their tracks are not easy to locate. There are four toes on each hand and three toes on each foot. The toes and fingers are short and stubby.

The foot, top, (50 mm) and hand (40 mm) of a rock hyrax; note the rubbery pads and the short toes.

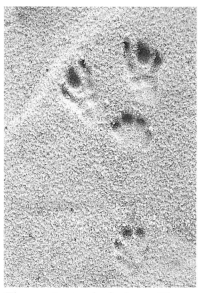

The running track of a hyrax. The foot tracks lie ahead of the hand prints. At first glance you could mistake this track for that of a hare or rabbit.

Track where a hyrax dragged its bottom; note the clear imprints of the feet at the top of the drag mark. This track is frequently seen and may have something to do with high internal parasite loads. The domestic dog also drags its bottom.

CLOVEN HOOFS

This large group of mammals includes the antelope, pigs, cattle, sheep and goats. They all walk on the tips of the third and fourth toes; the outer second and fifth toes are degenerate and play no part in locomotion. In a few species these dew-claws (false hoofs) may leave impressions in thick mud or deep sand; they include cattle, the buffalo, both wildebeest species and the bushpig.

The cloven hoof consists of two more or less equal parts. In nearly all cases the hoof tracks of the front feet are slightly larger than those of the hind feet. This is because the two halves of each front hoof tend to splay away from each other, whereas the reverse occurs in the case of the hind hoofs. Each hoof consists of a horny wall and an undersurface made up of the rubbery toe-pad and the harder sole. In soft ground the entire undersurface of the hoof leaves an imprint but on harder ground only the outer horny wall leaves a mark. Wherever possible we have included photographs of tracks on different ground surfaces.

We have placed the tracks in three broad size categories for convenience and where possible similar-sized species occurring in close association are described together. In most cases we have given only the length of the track left by the front foot. The hind foot track is usually smaller than the front. For several species we have shown examples to show variety

CLOVEN HOOFS – LARGE

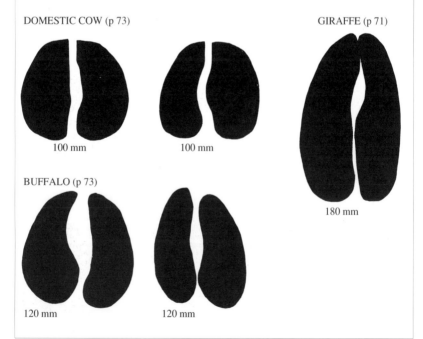

DOMESTIC COW (p 73)

100 mm

100 mm

GIRAFFE (p 71)

180 mm

BUFFALO (p 73)

120 mm

120 mm

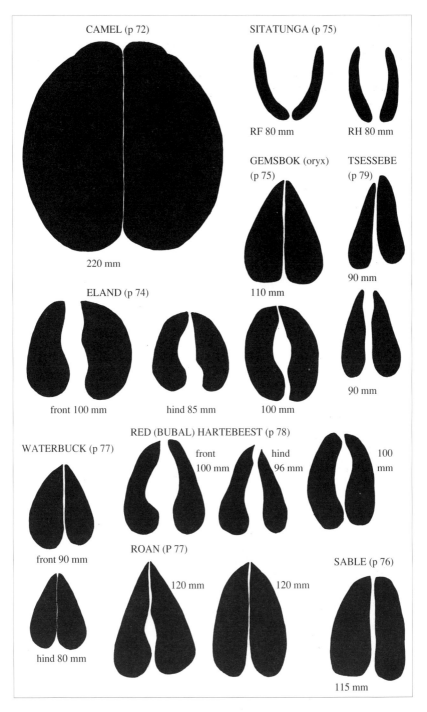

CAMEL (p 72)

220 mm

SITATUNGA (p 75)

RF 80 mm

RH 80 mm

GEMSBOK (oryx) (p 75)

110 mm

TSESSEBE (p 79)

90 mm

90 mm

ELAND (p 74)

front 100 mm

hind 85 mm

100 mm

WATERBUCK (p 77)

front 90 mm

hind 80 mm

RED (BUBAL) HARTEBEEST (p 78)

front 100 mm

hind 96 mm

100 mm

ROAN (P 77)

120 mm

120 mm

SABLE (p 76)

115 mm

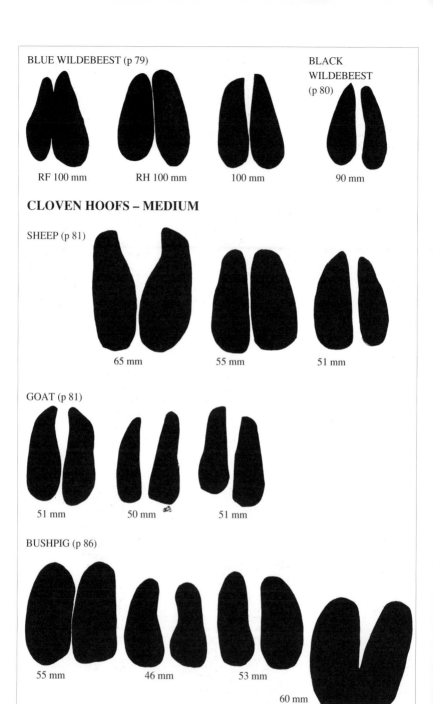

BLUE WILDEBEEST (p 79)

BLACK WILDEBEEST (p 80)

RF 100 mm   RH 100 mm   100 mm   90 mm

CLOVEN HOOFS – MEDIUM

SHEEP (p 81)

65 mm   55 mm   51 mm

GOAT (p 81)

51 mm   50 mm   51 mm

BUSHPIG (p 86)

55 mm   46 mm   53 mm

60 mm

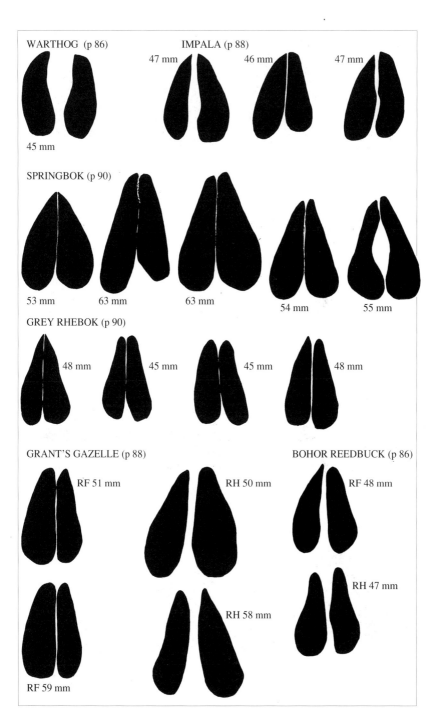

WARTHOG (p 86)

45 mm

IMPALA (p 88)

47 mm   46 mm   47 mm

SPRINGBOK (p 90)

53 mm   63 mm   63 mm   54 mm   55 mm

GREY RHEBOK (p 90)

48 mm   45 mm   45 mm   48 mm

GRANT'S GAZELLE (p 88)

RF 51 mm   RH 50 mm

RF 59 mm   RH 58 mm

BOHOR REEDBUCK (p 86)

RF 48 mm

RH 47 mm

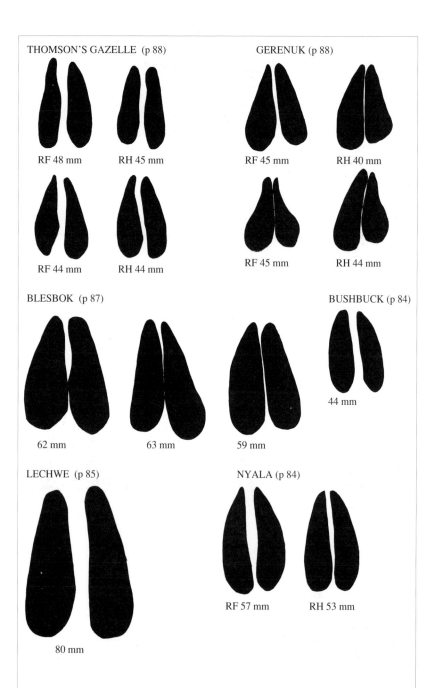

THOMSON'S GAZELLE (p 88)

RF 48 mm   RH 45 mm

RF 44 mm   RH 44 mm

GERENUK (p 88)

RF 45 mm   RH 40 mm

RF 45 mm   RH 44 mm

BLESBOK (p 87)

62 mm   63 mm   59 mm

BUSHBUCK (p 84)

44 mm

LECHWE (p 85)

80 mm

NYALA (p 84)

RF 57 mm   RH 53 mm

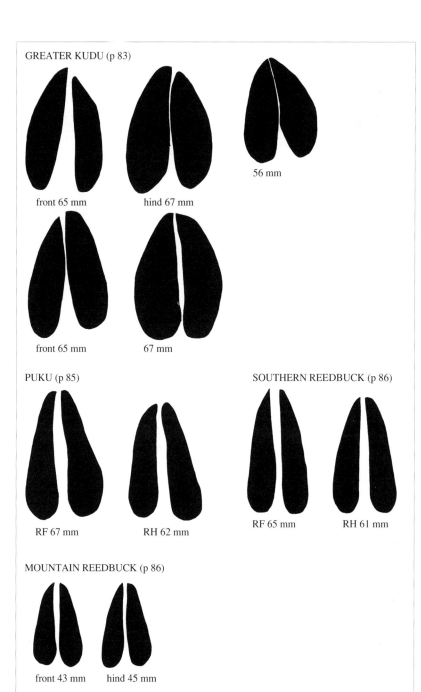

GREATER KUDU (p 83)

front 65 mm   hind 67 mm

56 mm

front 65 mm   67 mm

PUKU (p 85)

RF 67 mm   RH 62 mm

SOUTHERN REEDBUCK (p 86)

RF 65 mm   RH 61 mm

MOUNTAIN REEDBUCK (p 86)

front 43 mm   hind 45 mm

CLOVEN HOOFS – SMALL

COMMON DUIKER (p 92)

40 mm   42 mm

RED DUIKER (p 92)

30 mm

BLUE DUIKER (p 92)

front 24 mm   hind 22 mm

SHARPE'S GRYSBOK (p 93)

25 mm

CAPE GRYSBOK (p 93)

front 34 mm   hind 35 mm

KLIPSPRINGER

20 mm   21 mm

SUNI (p 93)

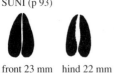

front 23 mm   hind 22 mm

DIK-DIK (p 94)

front 21 mm   hind 23 mm

STEENBOK (p 93)

front 39 mm   hind 40 mm   33 mm

ORIBI (p 93)

40 mm   42 mm

70

CLOVEN HOOFS – LARGE

GIRAFFE
This species has a wide but scattered distribution in woodland and savanna. The tracks are by far the largest of any in this group of animals (180-220 mm); we have measured some tracks almost 300 mm in length. The anterior edge of the track is rounded or even squared off.

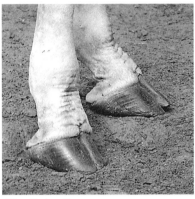

Giraffe hoofs.

Track of giraffe.

Giraffe tracks in fine river silt; hind footprint above.

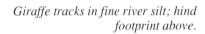

Always be alert for the unusual; this is the track of a giraffe that swivelled around 360° on being disturbed.

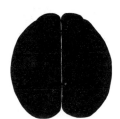

CAMEL
The toes of the camel are quite widely splayed, as an aid to walking in soft sand.

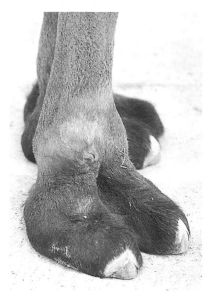

Front foot of a camel.

Front track of an adult camel (220 mm long and 220 mm wide). The tracks of the giraffe are much narrower and the hoof halves are distinct; both species occur in the same areas in northern Kenya.

COW, BUFFALO, ELAND
The tracks of these three ungulates are very similar in size and appearance (lengths are: domestic cow 100 mm; buffalo 120 mm; eland 100 mm). The tracks are somewhat rounded and the anterior edge is blunted. All three animals are widely distributed. Check which are present in the area where you find this type of track.

DOMESTIC COW

Cow track in soft ground.

Only the horny edge of the hoof leaves marks in hard substrates.

Cow tracks (bottom right), with sheep and common duiker tracks (left) in fine soil.

BUFFALO

Buffalo track in soft soil.

73

Buffalo tracks on hard ground, where only the horny hoof edge leaves an impression.

ELAND

front   hind

Eland track in soft ground.

Front hoof of an eland bull; note the rounded anterior edge.

Eland tracks in soft and hard ground.

RF   RH

SITATUNGA

The hoofs of the sitatunga are highly adapted to its swampy habitat and their tracks cannot be mistaken for those of any other species. You will not find these tracks away from the animal's watery habitat. The narrow, widely splayed front foot track (80 mm) and the slightly shorter and more closed hind track are diagnostic.

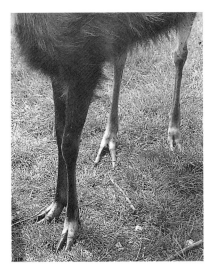

Here the hind track has partly registered on the front track.

The hoofs of a sitatunga ram, showing their great length and splaying.

GEMSBOK (ORYX)

Gemsbok populations occur in south-western and north-eastern African, in arid and semi-arid areas.

The front hoof of a gemsbok; note its heart shape and the pointed anterior edge.

Gemsbok front hoof track (average 110 mm).

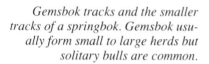

Gemsbok tracks and the smaller tracks of a springbok. Gemsbok usually form small to large herds but solitary bulls are common.

SABLE

The track measures 90-110 mm in length and the anterior edge is usually more pointed than in the similarly sized roan track. However, we have seen tracks of sable bulls that closely resembled those of roan. Sable occur in small herds but lone bulls are common.

Sable track in soft sand.

ROAN
The track of this large antelope could be mistaken for that of the sable and the eland where their distributions overlap. The track length ranges from 100-120 mm. The anterior track edge can be more rounded than that of the sable. Roan live in small herds.

Track of roan in sandy soil.

Left: *Roan tracks; note the different hoof impressions in soft and compacted sand.*

WATERBUCK
This species leaves a fairly sharply pointed, heart-shaped track (90 mm in length). The track is similar to that of the gemsbok but their distributions rarely overlap.

Waterbuck tracks in dry sand.

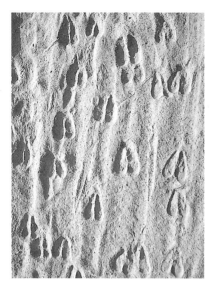

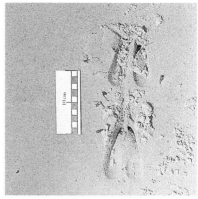

Tracks in damp sand that had caused slight splaying.

Left: *Tracks of several waterbuck in fine, dry river silt.*

RED (BUBAL) HARTEBEEST

front   hind

The tracks of the red and Lichtenstein's hartebeest are very similar but the ranges of the species do not overlap. Track length averages 80-100 mm and the inner edge of each hoof half is to some degree concave. Hartebeest are herding antelope.

Red hartebeest tracks.

Red hartebeest hoof; note the concave inner hoof edges and the rounded anterior edge.

TSESSEBE and TOPI
The tracks are similar to those of the hartebeest but they are narrower and shorter (75-90 mm).

Tsessebe tracks in damp ground.

BLUE WILDEBEEST
Populations occur in southern and east Africa and in some game parks this species is very common. Tracks average 100 mm in length and are wider than those of the red hartebeest.

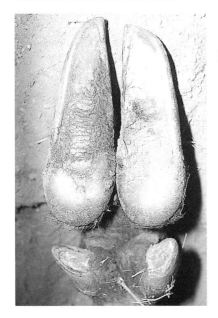

RF   RH

The front hoof of a blue wildebeest; note the low and well developed dew-claws.

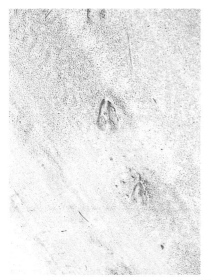

Blue wildebeest tracks showing the difference in the impressions in soft and hard ground.

BLACK WILDEBEEST
Tracks left by this species are similar to those of the blue wildebeest but on average shorter (90 mm), and the species do not occur naturally in the same areas. This wildebeest is restricted to the east-central interior of South Africa. The dew-claws are well developed and may show in soft ground.

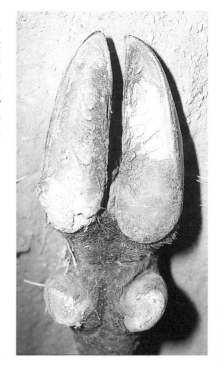

Hoof of a black wildebeest.

CLOVEN HOOFS – MEDIUM

This is a diverse group of antelope, pigs, domestic sheep and goats. All have tracks that do not exceed 80 mm in length but do exceed 40 mm. Remember that the tracks of young animals are smaller than those of adults.

SHEEP AND GOATS

These well-known domesticated animals can be encountered in most areas of Africa, with the exception of forest.

SHEEP

GOAT

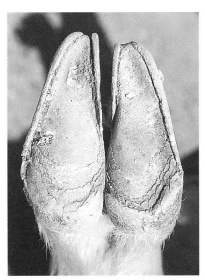

The hind hoof of a sheep is slightly more pointed.

Front hoof of a domestic sheep; note the somewhat rectangular shape and the blunt anterior edge.

Sheep tracks average 60 mm in length.

81

Goat tracks (average 52 mm) are very similar to those of sheep but they tend to be slightly smaller and the anterior edge is more pointed. However, goat and sheep tracks are often difficult to separate.

OKAPI AND BONGO

Both are tropical forest species and their ranges overlap in eastern Zaïre. The okapi is restricted to the forests of north-eastern Zaïre but the bongo occurs patchily in suitable habitat from West Africa through the Zaïre basin to isolated Kenyan montane forests

OKAPI

RF

Okapi track (average 75-85 mm)
(Photo: Roland van Bocxstaele).

BONGO

RH

Bongo track (average 75-85 mm)
(Photo: Roland van Bocxstaele).

82

GREATER AND LESSER KUDU

The greater kudu occurs widely in southern and east Africa but the lesser kudu is restricted to the latter region. Both kudu live in various woodland habitats.

The lesser kudu inhabits dry bush and thicket country in northern Tanzania, Kenya, north-eastern Uganda and extending into the Horn of Africa. The tracks are similar to those of the greater kudu (see page 69) but smaller. Solitary individuals, particularly rams, are commonly seen but small groups of three to five individuals are usual. Their droppings are deposited at random within their home range.

The front hoof of a greater kudu (55-80 mm) showing the typical oval form.

A track of a greater kudu in fine sand. The neat and compact track is easy to identify.

GREATER KUDU

Greater kudu track.

83

NYALA

This antelope has a limited distribution in south-eastern Africa. It is abundant in the parks of northern Natal (South Africa). The tracks are similar to those of the bushbuck but tracks left by the nyala bull are larger (50-60 mm); those of the nyala ewe and the bushbuck ram are similar in size.

RF   RH

BUSHBUCK

This is one of the most widespread African antelope and it occurs in a wide range of forest and woodland habitats. Its tracks (front length 40-50 mm) could be confused with those of nyala where their ranges overlap but this occurs in only a few areas in south-eastern Africa.

The front hoof of a bushbuck.

KOB, PUKU, RED LECHWE

The kob and puku are considered by some authorities to be the same species and the structure and length of the hoofs are inseparable. The tracks of the kob and puku measure 55-70 mm. Red lechwe tracks range from 70-80 mm in length. These species occur on floodplains and marshland fringes.

LECHWE   PUKU

 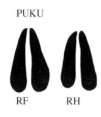

RF   RH

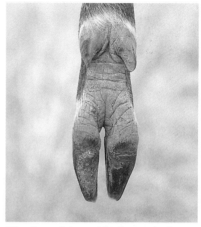

The feet of the red lechwe are characterised by the absence of hair up to the dew-claws, an adaptation to the swampy ground on which they spend much of their time. The hoofs are elongated but not to the same extent as those of the sitatunga.

Puku tracks.

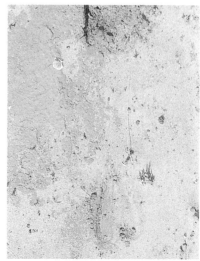

On soft ground the hoofs of the red lechwe splay to achieve better purchase but on hard ground this is not usually evident.

85

MOUNTAIN, SOUTHERN and BOHOR REEDBUCK

Isolated populations of mountain reedbuck occur in mountains and hill country in south-eastern and east Africa. The track averages 45 mm in length and could be confused with the track of the grey rhebok where these species occur together in the south.

The other two species occupy river floodplains, reedbeds and flooded grasslands but they are largely separated by different distribution patterns. The track of the southern reedbuck averages 65 mm and that of the bohor reedbuck is slightly smaller.

SOUTHERN REEDBUCK   MOUNTAIN REEDBUCK

front 43 mm

RF 65 mm   RH 61 mm

hind 45 mm

BOHOR REEDBUCK

 RF 45 mm   RH 47 mm

Bohor reedbuck walking tracks.

BUSHPIG, GIANT FOREST HOG, WARTHOG

The bushpig and the warthog occur widely in sub-Saharan Africa but the former occupies forest, dense woodland and thickets whereas the latter lives in open woodland and savanna. The giant forest hog overlaps with the bushpig in parts of the equatorial forest block and both live in sounders. The hog has larger tracks but it is difficult to separate the two forest dwellers. The track of the bushpig averages 55 mm in length but we have seen imprints of large boars that measured over 70 mm. Warthog tracks are smaller (length 48 mm) and the dew-claws do not show in soft substrate, whereas they frequently do in the other two species. The hoofs of the warthog are also narrower.

BUSHPIG   WARTHOG

The "square" track of a bushpig.

86

BONTEBOK and BLESBOK

This species (the bontebok and blesbok are subspecies) is restricted to the coastal plain of the south-western Cape and the interior grassland plains of South Africa. The track length ranges from 60-70 mm.

BLESBOK

Bontebok track in sandy substrate.

Track in hardening mud; note that only the impressions of the horny layer left a mark.

Splayed track in soft mud.

GERENUK, GRANT'S GAZELLE, THOMSON'S GAZELLE, IMPALA

All four species occur in east Africa but only the impala is found in southern Africa. They all show a marked preference for open savanna woodland. Only the Grant's gazelle and the gerenuk overlap to any extent.

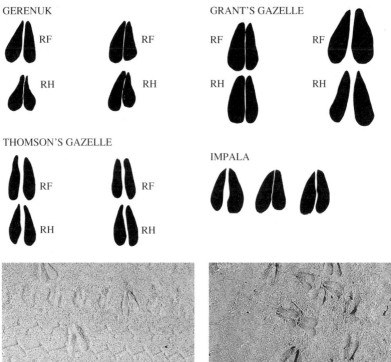

Gerenuk tracks; front prints average 45 mm in length and hind tracks 40-44 mm. This antelope may be encountered singly or in groups of up to five.

Grant's gazelle tracks in damp mud (front 50-58 mm in length; hind 50-59 mm).

Grant's gazelle tracks in fine sand. This species occurs in east Africa.

Thomson's gazelle tracks (front 44-46 mm in length; hind 42-44 mm). This small antelope is restricted to southern Kenya and northern Tanzania.

Impala tracks criss-crossing to and from a waterhole. Impala tracks measure 45-52 mm in length.

SPRINGBOK

This antelope has a neat, sharp-pointed, heart-shaped track (average length 55 mm). Springbok are restricted to the arid south-west of southern Africa and live in herds, although solitary rams are common.

A springbok track; note the neat, heart shape of the track.

A set of springbok walking tracks; note the striped polecat tracks on the right.

GREY RHEBOK

The rather long (45 mm) and narrow track distinguishes it from that of the mountain reedbuck with which the grey rhebok shares its range in southern Africa.

The front and hind hoofs of a grey rhebok.

Track of the front hoof; note its length compared to width.

The narrow track of a grey rhebok (right). Compare with the bontebok track (top) and that of the common duiker (bottom left).

DUIKERS

Most duiker species occupy forest and dense woodland, or their fringes, and occur in the tropical forest belt, but the red duiker and the blue duiker occur both within this zone and outside it as far south as South Africa. The track of the blue duiker ranges from 17-25 mm but that of the red duiker is larger at 22-34 mm. The common (Grimm's) duiker shows a preference for scrub and lightly bushed country but in some areas occupies forest fringes. The tracks are compact and heart-shaped and range in length from 28-40 mm.

COMMON DUIKER

RED DUIKER

BLUE DUIKER

front   hind

The front and hind hoofs of the common (Grimm's) duiker.

Track of the front hoof of a common duiker.

ROYAL ANTELOPE

This tiny, delicate antelope inhabits the equatorial forest zone. The tracks are rarely longer than 15 mm but they could be confused with those of the small duikers.

SUNI

The tracks of the suni average 22 mm in length and they could be confused with those of the blue duiker where the two species occur together.

ORIBI and STEENBOK

Both species occur in grassland and open woodland; in south-eastern and east Africa their ranges overlap. Their tracks are very similar but are longer in the oribi (32-40 mm) than in the steenbok (30 - 38 mm). The steenbok is solitary but the oribi occurs in groups of three to five.

ORIBI

STEENBOK

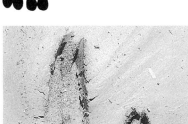

Tracks of a steenbok; this animal lived in an area dominated by loose sands and its hoofs were consequently longer than usual. The possibility of this adaptation should always be borne in mind when you are looking at antelope tracks in sandy areas.

CAPE GRYSBOK (GRYSBOK), SHARPE'S GRYSBOK

The tracks of the Cape grysbok (25-35 mm in length) are similar to those of the common duiker. The Cape grysbok is a solitary species that inhabits low but dense bush along the coast of the Cape Province (South Africa). Sharpe's grysbok is restricted to east and south-eastern Africa and occupies thickets. Sharpe's grysbok tracks are smaller than those of the Cape grysbok (24-26 mm). In some areas the Sharpe's grysbok and the suni overlap; the tracks of the suni (average length 22 mm) are very similar but slightly narrower. This

CAPE GRYSBOK

SHARPE'S GRYSBOK

is a case where you would have to look for other signs, such as latrine sites, which may lead you to an identification.

Front track of Cape grysbok.

DIK-DIK
The tracks of the different dik-dik species are very similar. The track length of the Damara (Kirk's) dik-dik is 21-23 mm. In the south-west Damara dik-dik tracks should not be confused with those of any other species but in east Africa you also have to take into account Sharpe's grysbok and the suni. Dik-dik tracks are usually more pointed than those of the other two species.

 front   hind

KLIPSPRINGER
Klipspringer tracks are arguably the easiest antelope tracks to identify as each individual track consists of two oval, widely separated "slots". Klipspringers inhabit rocky terrain in association with mountains and hills, and tracks may be found in valleys between the hills and along stream banks. Individual "slots" measure 15-20 mm in length.

An example of a klipspringer hoof slot.

NON-CLOVEN HOOFS

This group includes the horse, the donkey and the zebras. The general hoof structure is well known. These are all members of the horse family; they have only one toe (the third) on each leg and only the "tip" of the toe comes into contact with the ground. A well developed hoof extends over the edge of the toe-pad, or frog.

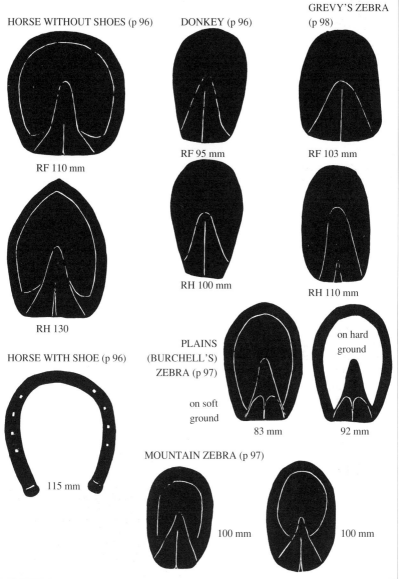

HORSE WITHOUT SHOES (p 96)

RF 110 mm

RH 130

HORSE WITH SHOE (p 96)

115 mm

DONKEY (p 96)

RF 95 mm

RH 100 mm

PLAINS (BURCHELL'S) ZEBRA (p 97)

on soft ground

83 mm

on hard ground

92 mm

GREVY'S ZEBRA (p 98)

RF 103 mm

RH 110 mm

MOUNTAIN ZEBRA (p 97)

100 mm

100 mm

HORSE and DONKEY

The front hoof is roughly circular in the horse with an indentation on the posterior edge; the hind hoof is more elongated. The size of the hoofs varies from breed to breed. Donkey tracks are shorter and more slender than horse tracks, more closely resembling those of Hartmann's and Cape mountain zebras.

HORSE WITHOUT
SHOES

RF

RH

HORSE WITH
SHOE

HORSE WITH
SHOE

DONKEY

RF

RH

Left: *Front hoof of a horse; note the way the hoof extends over the frog, which is only visible as a triangle of darker tissue. Also see how the outer edge of the hoof is slightly raised: this is the only part that leaves a mark on hard ground.* Right: *Hind hoof of the same horse; it is visibly narrower than the front hoof.*

Imprint of a hind hoof of a horse with the triangular frog clearly visible.

96

PLAINS (BURCHELL'S) ZEBRA

This is the most widespread of the zebra species in southern and east Africa. The tracks resemble those of a small horse, with the front hoof tracks being rounder than the hind. Track length is 120-140 mm; the hind track is usually slightly longer but narrower. However, as in horse tracks there is considerable variation.

 on soft ground

 on hard ground

A front zebra track registering over a hind track.

Plains zebra tracks.

HARTMANN'S ZEBRA and CAPE MOUNTAIN ZEBRA

These zebras are sub-species and their tracks are identical. Both the front and hind tracks are noticeably narrower than those of the plains zebra, and could be confused with donkey tracks. Length range of the track is 110-138 mm. Hartmann's zebra overlaps marginally with the plains zebra in north-western Namibia, otherwise their distributions are mutually exclusive. Hartmann's zebra occurs along the length of the

97

Namibian escarpment and the Cape mountain zebra is restricted to a few reserves in South Africa.

Hartmann's zebra track in soft sand.

Hartmann's zebra track on hard ground, showing only the horny hoof edge. Note the tracks of a springbok right.

GREVY'S ZEBRA

This species is restricted to a few small populations in Kenya and further north, but its range overlaps with that of the plains zebra in some areas. The tracks are narrower than those of the plains zebra.

RF

RH

The tracks of Grevy's zebra (front 103 mm long, 80 mm wide; hind 110 mm long, 70 mm wide); the upper clear print was left by a front hoof. The tiny cloven-hoof prints of a Damara dik-dik lead from left to right.

THREE TOES VISIBLE

Only two species fall into this group, the springhare and the aardvark (antbear), and they cannot be confused. Although both species have more than three toes on each foot, the track normally leaves clear impressions of only three toes. The springhare hops on its hind feet but the aardvark walks on all fours.

SPRINGHARE (p 100)

L   R

on soft ground 38 mm

on hard ground
(note claws) 51 mm

sitting 102 mm

AARDVARK (p 101)

RF 100 mm (with claws)

RH 90 mm (with claws)

SPRINGHARE

This strange kangaroo-like rodent hops on the hind legs and the front feet usually come into contact with the ground only when the animal is feeding. The hind feet are equipped with four toes, each with stout claws, but only three show clearly in the track. The claws are roughly diamond-shaped, with the middle claw being the longest. This animal is widespread in southern and east Africa. In suitable sandy grassland areas it is very common and may occur in high densities.

on soft ground 38 mm

 on hard ground
(note claws)

sitting

The hind foot of a springhare; note the heavy claws on the toes. Normally only 40-75 mm of the hind foot comes into contact with the ground but when the animal is sitting the full length of the hind foot may leave an impression (up to 145 mm). If the animal is moving at speed only the claws come into contact with the ground.

A series of paired tracks of a springhare. An animal at full speed may leave a distance between tracks of as much as 1,8 m.

Hind foot tracks of a springhare in the sitting position (left centre); the other tracks are of baboons.

AARDVARK (ANTBEAR)

Although the front foot has four toes and the hind foot five, only three toes on each foot always show clearly in the track. This species occurs throughout sub-Saharan Africa and is found wherever there are adequate numbers of termites, which form the bulk of its food. The aardvark is a solitary species.

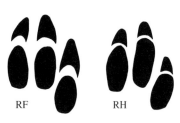

RF   RH

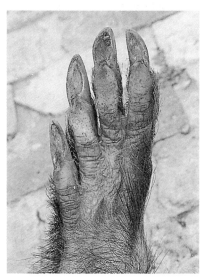

The front foot of an aardvark; note the massive claws on the toes.

Track of the front foot of an aardvark in mud. Most tracks measure 80-100 mm but we have encountered tracks with a length of 130 mm.

Aardvark front foot track in sand; the indentations of the claws are clearly visible.

101

BIG GAME

The feet of the hippopotamus, the two rhinoceros species and the elephant are huge and adapted to carry massive bulk. The hippopotamus and the elephant have wide distributions in sub-Saharan Africa but the rhinoceros species are restricted to reserves, mainly in southern Africa.

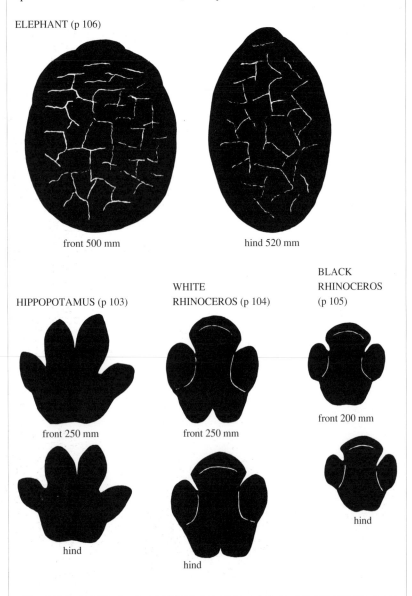

ELEPHANT (p 106)

front 500 mm

hind 520 mm

HIPPOPOTAMUS (p 103)

WHITE RHINOCEROS (p 104)

BLACK RHINOCEROS (p 105)

front 250 mm

front 250 mm

front 200 mm

hind

hind

hind

HIPPOPOTAMUS

This semi-aquatic giant has four rounded toes on each foot, the tips being encased in a horny hoof. Each track ranges from 230-280 mm in length. The tracks do not resemble those of any other species. In the forests of west Africa one could encounter the pygmy hippopotamus, whose tracks are similar but much smaller.

front

hind

The hippopotamus has a wide straddle and in soft ground two shallow trenches develop in regularly used tracks. This can be clearly seen in the photograph.

Hippopotamus tracks in different substrates.

WHITE (SQUARE-LIPPED) RHINOCEROS

Both rhinoceros species have three horny-nailed toes, the largest in front and a slightly smaller one on either side. The front foot track is slightly more rounded than the hind track and averages 300 mm in length. The hind foot track is usually narrower than the front and may be slightly shorter. The tracks of this species are larger than those of the black (hook-lipped) rhino and the indentation on the posterior edge is usually more pronounced. The white rhino is found mainly in southern African reserves and on game farms.

front

hind

White rhino front foot track; note the lines left by the sole and the clear nail impressions.

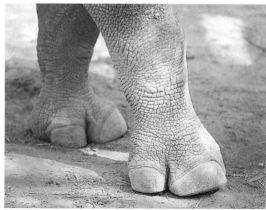

The front foot of a white rhino.

Hind foot track; it is narrower and shorter than the front track.

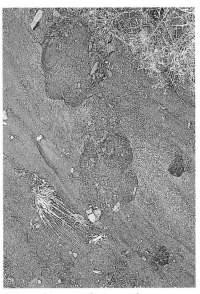

White rhino tracks in mud.

BLACK (HOOK-LIPPED) RHINOCEROS

The tracks are very similar to those of the white rhino but shorter (180-240 mm). They also may show the mosaic of cracks under the feet in fine soil. The indentation on the posterior edge is usually not well pronounced.

front

hind

Front (above) and hind tracks of a black rhino.

ELEPHANT

The tracks of the elephant are huge and cannot be mistaken for those of any other species. The track of the front foot is almost circular with a diameter of about 500 mm (remember that you may observe the tracks of younger and therefore smaller animals in a herd). The hind foot track is more oval in shape. Fresh tracks in fine silt or sand show a clear mosaic of criss-crossed ridges and furrows.

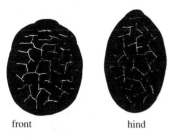

front   hind

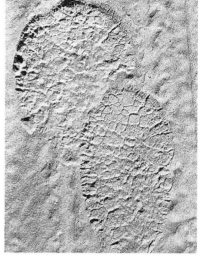

Fresh elephant tracks, on the left the rounded front imprint, with the more oval hind track slightly registered on it. Note the characteristic mosaic of ridges and furrows.

Older elephant tracks overlaid with bird and insect tracks; the wind has levelled the mosaic of ridges.

Tracks that are more than three months old. They were pressed in wet mud and would remain intact until the following rainy season.

Fresh elephant trail through grass; the approximate impressions of the feet can still be seen.

Some elephant-created paths may already have been in use for hundreds, if not thousands, of years, such as this one in northern Botswana.

BIRD AND OTHER TRACKS

With a few exceptions, it is very difficult to identify birds to species level on tracks alone. We have selected a few typical examples from the major foot types and these should help you at least to place a track in a family or similar group. Birds walk on their toes and the heel is held well clear of the ground. There are never more than four toes (three forward and one back), sometimes there are three forward-pointing and in the case of the ostrich only two forward-pointing toes. In nearly all cases each toe carries a claw at its tip, ranging from the long and well developed talons of the birds of prey to the poorly developed claws of the ducks and geese. Many swimming birds have webbing between the toes and this may be visible in the track. The smaller birds, such as robins, thrushes, buntings and larks, may move on the ground by walking or hopping.

When you try to identify a bird track first measure its total length. Then look at whether there is a back toe (if so, is it long, short or bent to the side?); are the toes long or short, are they stout or slender, is there webbing between the toes? Look at the following photographs and drawings which may help you to reach an identification.

WEBBED FEET

THREE OBVIOUS FORWARD-POINTING TOES
This group includes the ducks and geese, gulls, flamingoes and the avocet. In some cases a tiny back toe (first toe) may leave a slight impression in the track. Webbing is an aid to swimming.

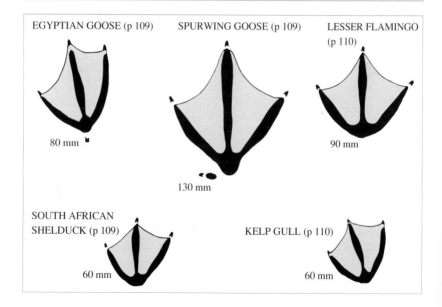

EGYPTIAN GOOSE (p 109)
80 mm

SPURWING GOOSE (p 109)
130 mm

LESSER FLAMINGO (p 110)
90 mm

SOUTH AFRICAN SHELDUCK (p 109)
60 mm

KELP GULL (p 110)
60 mm

Webbing on the feet of geese and ducks extends from toe-tip to toe-tip; this belongs to a spurwing goose.

Tracks of an Egyptian goose; note how the front turns inward to give the track a "pigeon-toed" appearance.

Shelduck tracks; the webbing can be clearly seen. All geese and ducks have the "pigeon-toed" walking style.

Walking sequence of a shelduck.

Kelp gull tracks on firm sand in which the webbing is not visible. Gulls also have a "pigeon-toed" walking style.

Individual flamingo tracks are difficult to isolate because many birds usually occur together, but the feeding tracks, shown here, are characteristic.

Lesser flamingo tracks; note the clear lines left by the webbing.

The avocet has webbing between the toes but this seldom shows clearly in the track, so look out for typical feeding signs such as these.

FOUR OBVIOUS TOES

Species in this group include the pelicans, cormorants, coots and grebes. The type and extent of the webbing vary.

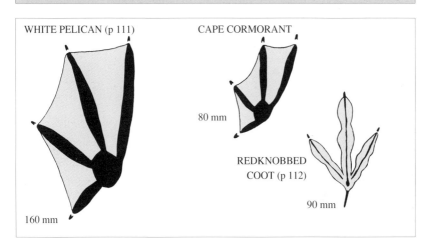

WHITE PELICAN (p 111)

CAPE CORMORANT

80 mm

REDKNOBBED COOT (p 112)

90 mm

160 mm

The feet of a white pelican showing its long toes and extensive webbing. Three toes are forward-pointing and one shorter toe is angled inwards.

The "pigeon-toed" tracks of a white pelican; note that the webbing is not visible in compact sand.

The scalloped webbing of a coot which leaves a distinctive track.

FEET WITHOUT WEBBING

THREE TOES FORWARD; NO BACK TOE
This group includes the dikkops, coursers, plovers, bustards and korhaans, the blue and wattled cranes, sandgrouse and many of the resident and migratory waders. Wader tracks look alike but vary greatly in size. Although a few species in this group have a small back toe, it rarely comes into contact with the ground.

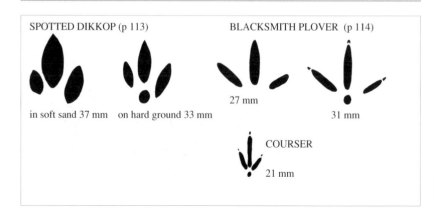

SPOTTED DIKKOP (p 113)

in soft sand 37 mm   on hard ground 33 mm

BLACKSMITH PLOVER (p 114)

27 mm

31 mm

COURSER

21 mm

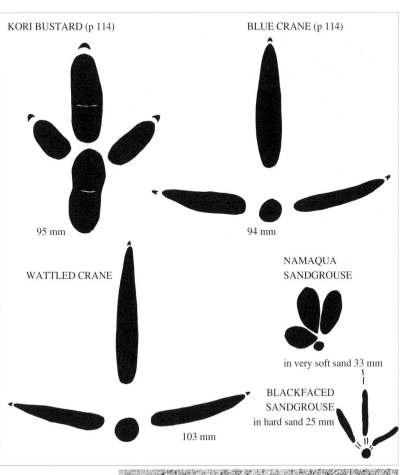

KORI BUSTARD (p 114)

BLUE CRANE (p 114)

95 mm

94 mm

WATTLED CRANE

NAMAQUA
SANDGROUSE

in very soft sand 33 mm

BLACKFACED
SANDGROUSE
in hard sand 25 mm

103 mm

*Spotted dikkop
track in mud.*

113

Tracks of a blacksmith plover.

Kori bustard track showing the stout toes, blunt claws and the extension to the rear; this is not a toe.

The foot of a blue crane; note how the back toe is not in contact with the ground.

When bustards and korhaans are walking the central toe frequently leaves a distinct drag mark. These tracks are of a Ludwig's bustard.

The three-toed tracks of curlew sandpipers.

Tracks of a blackfaced sandgrouse; all sandgrouse tracks are similar. Note how the claw of the middle toe leaves a distinct drag mark.

THREE TOES FORWARD; BACK TOE ANGLED

This group includes the francolins, partridges, guineafowl, the white and marabou storks and the crowned crane. The back toe is usually short (but in some cases fairly long) and pointing to the side at a variable angle.

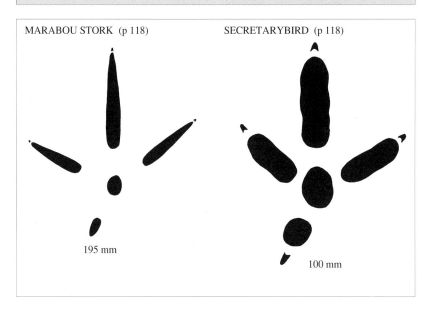

MARABOU STORK (p 118)

195 mm

SECRETARYBIRD (p 118)

100 mm

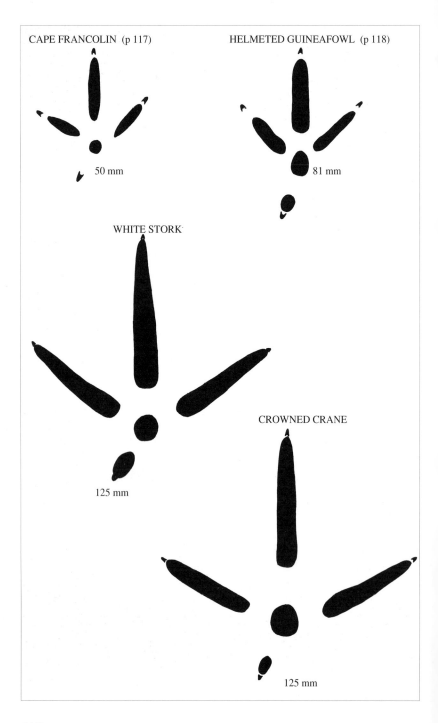

CAPE FRANCOLIN (p 117)

50 mm

HELMETED GUINEAFOWL (p 118)

81 mm

WHITE STORK

125 mm

CROWNED CRANE

125 mm

The foot of a male Cape francolin; note the three well developed front toes and the short back toe. The spur above the back toe does not come into contact with the ground.

The walking trail of a redbilled francolin which clearly shows the track of the short, angled back toe. This is typical of all francolin species.

Track of a Natal francolin; note how the toes have created drag marks.

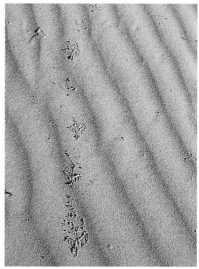

Cape francolin tracks on dew-dampened sand.

Helmeted guineafowl tracks showing claw marks and short, angled back toe.

Helmeted guineafowl trail.

The back toe of the marabou stork is not always angled, as in this case.

Track of a secretarybird; note the shallow indentation left by the short back toe but the distinct mark left by the claw. The track is similar to those of the bustards but they lack a back toe.

THREE TOES FORWARD; BACK TOE STRAIGHT

This group includes the vast majority of birds species and we can do little more than give a few examples.

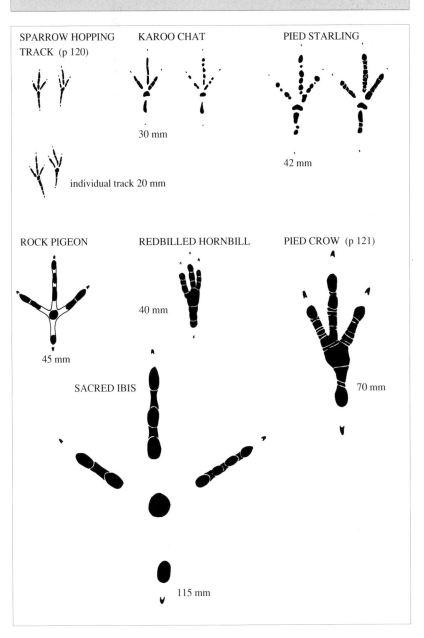

SPARROW HOPPING TRACK (p 120)

KAROO CHAT

30 mm

individual track 20 mm

PIED STARLING

42 mm

ROCK PIGEON

45 mm

REDBILLED HORNBILL

40 mm

SACRED IBIS

115 mm

PIED CROW (p 121)

70 mm

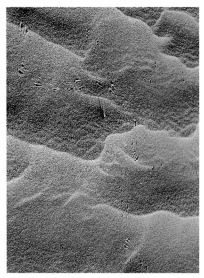

Many small birds, such as the sparrows and buntings, hop with both feet, leaving paired tracks.

Hopping and walking tracks of larks foraging.

Tracks of a foraging Cape wagtail.

Olive thrush trail.

Pied crow tracks.

THREE TOES FORWARD; BACK TOE OFF-CENTRE
Several of the herons have three long, forward-pointing toes and one long back toe that lies slightly off-centre. In our experience the position of the back toe is variable even within the same species and on occasion it is even centred: most confusing!

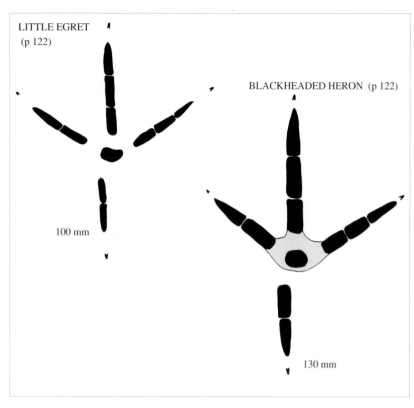

LITTLE EGRET
(p 122)

100 mm

BLACKHEADED HERON (p 122)

130 mm

Blackheaded heron track clearly showing the off-centre back toe.

The tracks of a little egret; note that some tracks show the back toe off-centre but in others it is centred. These tracks were left by the same bird!

This group includes the owls, parrots and woodpeckers. Few of the species spend much time on the ground and tracks are therefore seldom found.

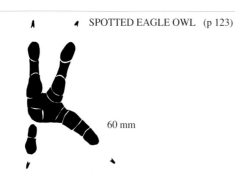

SPOTTED EAGLE OWL   (p 123)

60 mm

Foot of a spotted eagle owl showing the position of the toes.

Track of a spotted eagle owl (left) with white-tailed mongoose and hartebeest tracks.

123

TWO TOES FORWARD, NONE BACK

The ostrich is a unique African bird in that it only has two forward-pointing toes. The track cannot be mistaken for any other.

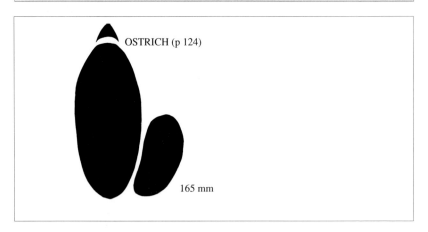

OSTRICH (p 124)

165 mm

Foot of an ostrich; note the large toe armed with a stout nail.

Track of an ostrich.

"TRAMLINE" TRAIL

We include the tortoises, terrapins, the Nile crocodile, frogs, crabs and invertebrates in this section, which consequently encompasses dozens of different tracks; we have chosen as examples those that we have encountered most frequently. Species identification from tracks alone is seldom possible. "Tramline" indicates that the tracks of the right and left sides of the animal are clearly separated.

The trail of an angulate tortoise in rain-dampened sand.

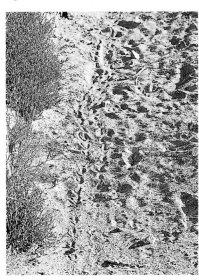

Tortoise trail along fence-line in soft sand.

Individual tracks of tortoises are seldom clear but when they are found they often show the marks left by the scalation and claws shown here.

125

Terrapin trails in thin mud.

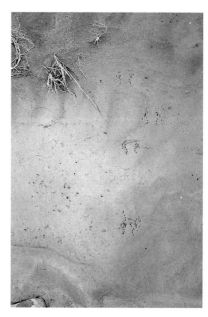

The hopping trail of a frog known as a dwarf pyxie; note that it does not strictly fit the "tramline" definition. Toads when hopping leave a similar trail.

The track of a rain frog (Breviceps sp) in damp sand.

The trail of a ghost crab; these crabs are common on African beaches.

126

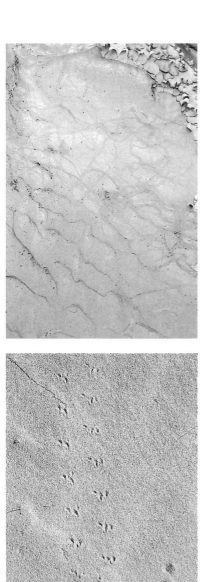

A maze of millipede trails in damp mud.

The trail of a flightless Tenebrionid beetle. Most beetles have a similar trail.

A baboon spider trail leading from left to right.

The track of a cricket on a dune slope.

"TRAMLINE" TRAIL WITH CENTRAL DRAG MARK

This group includes most of the lizards and the scorpions. Species identification from tracks alone is seldom possible.

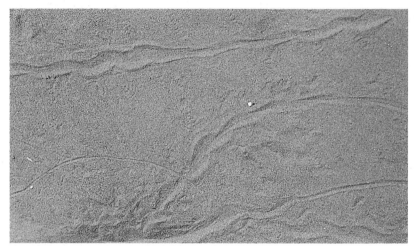

When lizards sun themselves, they usually flatten their bodies against the substrate and leave distinct marks.

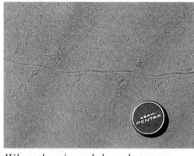

When the air and the substrate warm up lizards raise themselves off the ground, leaving only the feet and tail in contact.

The tracks and tail drag mark of a large Nile monitor.

The undersurface of the feet of the monitor lizards are ridged and this may show in the track.

Nile monitor footprints; note the ridged toe tracks and the absence of a tail drag mark in this case.

Scorpions usually walk with the tail raised off the ground but on occasion the tail leaves a distinct drag mark.

UNDULATING TRACK WITHOUT FOOT MARKS
This group includes the tracks of invertebrates, certain mammals and reptiles. Species identification from tracks alone is seldom possible.

The undersurface trail of a beetle larva. This trail was about 10 mm across but you may encounter such trails of 3-20 mm in width. The trails may occur in mud, damp ground and even dry sand.

The meandering trails of antlion larvae seeking out new ground for excavating their conical pits.

The trail of a legless lizard on the slope of a sand dune.

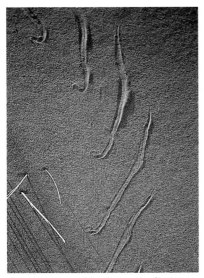

Peringuey's adder leaves a distinct side-winding trail. This species is found only on dune slopes in the Namib Desert.

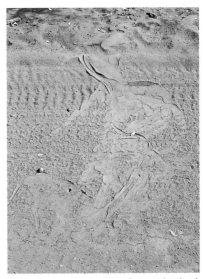

The place where a black mamba had been sunning itself on a sand track. Snake tracks on their own seldom allow for a species identification. We could identify this species because we saw the snake.

The trail of an Egyptian cobra – this can be taken as a typical snake trail. The puff adder when undisturbed moves in a straight line and the tail tip usually leaves a thin drag mark in the centre of the trail. Pythons may leave a similar trail to that of the puff adder.

The track of a striped sand snake.

Top and right: *Surface feeding trails of the Grant's (Namib) golden mole. It feeds at night and the foraging trails may be extensive.*

The domed surface tunnel of a Hottentot golden mole; several golden mole species excavate such foraging tunnels.

4 DROPPINGS AND BIRD PELLETS

Before you look at the photographs first consult the key in order to narrow down your search for the identification of droppings. Once you think you are on the right track turn to the relevant photographs to see whether your sample can be placed in that particular group. Although the shape, size and structure of the droppings are important, it is also of great help to take a close look at the location, number of droppings present, their content and any other signs close by such as tracks or food remains.

Most people initially turn their noses up when one starts to discuss the delights of droppings as an aid to species identification. When it is suggested that one should examine the contents of droppings, those with weaker stomachs tend to pale. But by examining the contents of carnivore droppings and bird pellets we are not only able to see what the individual has eaten but we can compile comprehensive information on the diet of a particular species from samples collected over several seasons.

Droppings consist of indigestible animal or plant material that may be deposited at random throughout the animal's home range, in strategic spots to act as territorial "signposts", or at latrine sites where large numbers of droppings may accumulate. Many mammal species have scent glands close to the anus and when droppings are deposited, secretion from these glands adheres to them. The secretion of each species has a distinctive smell. These scents are so complex that they impart information on the territory of an individual, its sexual state and its movements. Unfortunately this is of no use to a

Ground hornbills fragmenting elephant droppings to extract insects attracted to the dung. A wide range of birds and mammals feed from elephant dung. They may extract insects or seeds and other undigested plant parts.

KEY TO DROPPINGS

TINY CYLINDRICAL PELLETS (p 136)

SPHERICAL OR CYLINDRICAL PELLETS (p 138)

LOZENGE-SHAPED PELLETS (p 148)

GROOVED AND UNGROOVED, FLATTENED PELLETS (p 150)

DROPPINGS OF MIXED SHAPE AND FORM (p 150)

SAUSAGE-SHAPED, POINTED AT ONE END (p 154)

SAUSAGE-SHAPED, TAPERED AT ONE END AND USUALLY SEGMENTED (p 159)

KIDNEY-SHAPED (p 163)

THICK, "PANCAKE-LIKE" (p 165)

LARGE, BARREL-SHAPED (p 166)

FORMED SAUSAGE, POINTED AT BOTH ENDS, WITH HARD WHITISH CAP (p 173)

FORMED SAUSAGE, WITH PARTIAL WHITE COATING (p 172)

LIQUID DROPPINGS (p 169)

Termites in the process of breaking down rhino droppings.

Elephant droppings almost completely consumed by termites, although the approximate shape is retained.

human investigator and we have to rely on our sight to reach an identification.

Animals that eat plant food tend to produce larger quantities of droppings than do carnivorous and insectivorous species. The type and condition of food affect the form that droppings take. For example, herbivores (plant-eaters) feeding on dry, fibrous vegetation usually produce hard, compact droppings but those consuming lush, green plants often produce softer droppings.

The droppings and urine of mammals are excreted through two separate openings (anus and urethra), but birds and reptiles excrete wastes through one opening, the cloaca. In the case of birds the urine is usually whitish and cloaks all or part of the faeces, depending on the species. The droppings of most reptiles have a hard cap of uric acid. More details are given in the captions of the photographs that follow.

Many circumstances dictate for how long droppings remain intact and retain their original form. Droppings may be eaten by another species (spotted hyaena, for example, may consume fresh dung of lion and wild dog); droppings may be broken up and scattered by animals searching for dung beetles and other insects; termites frequently fragment the droppings of elephant and other herbivores and dung beetles soon break up the dung of such species as buffalo and cattle.

Dung beetles preparing brood and food balls from buffalo dung. These balls may be either rolled away to be buried or buried at the site of the dung.

135

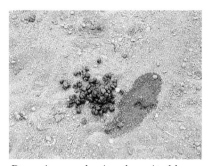

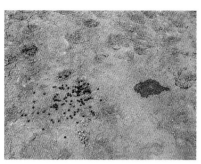

Droppings and urine deposited by an impala ewe. Note that the droppings are closely clustered because the ewe squats when defecating.

Droppings and urine deposited by an impala ram. As the ram does not squat, or squats less than the ewe, the dung pellets are more scattered.

It is often possible to identify the sex of an animal by the position of the droppings in relation to the urine splash mark. The male's urine is deposited well forward of the droppings and lies between the tracks left by the front and hind feet (or slightly to the side). The urine deposited by the female lies close to the droppings and between or just behind the tracks of the hind feet. It should be noted, however, that in some species (for example rhinos) the male expels the urine backwards.

Single pellets or small accumulations of tiny cylindrical pellets

This type of dropping is produced by the insect-eating bats and the small rodent species. It is virtually impossible to distinguish bat species by droppings alone. Although similar to mouse droppings, bat droppings crush more easily and consist entirely of insect fragments. Most measure 5-12 mm in length and large accumulations of droppings can be found at the bats' day-time roosts; in cave roosts where many thousands of bats may gather tons of droppings accumulate. Some species roost in buildings. Scattered bat droppings are frequently found on house porches below lights where the bats hunt insects at night. Remember that these little creatures are catching large numbers of potentially harmful insects around your house; reflect on this when you grumble about having to sweep up after your nocturnal visitors!

136

Droppings of the Egyptian slit-faced bat and the Cape serotine bat.

Droppings of Cape serotine bats at the entrance to their roost.

Like the droppings of the insectivorous bats, those of the small rodents are all very similar. In most cases droppings are deposited at random as the animal moves about, but a number of species drop their dung pellets at latrine sites. The pellets are 3-15 mm in length and range in colour from black to pale brown. Accumulations of rodent droppings may be found in buildings and food storage facilities, on and below dry-stone walls, in rock crevices and among dense vegetation such as grass tussocks, sedge meadows (vlei rats) and scrub tangles.

A selection of typical rodent droppings, clockwise from top left: vlei rat (Otomys spp), spectacled dormouse, Namaqua rock mouse, house mouse, tree mouse, striped mouse, dassie rat.

The dassie rat occurs in rocky terrain in the arid west of southern Africa. They deposit their droppings in small latrine areas at the entrances to narrow rock crevices. Dry white urine deposits are always present. Compare the photographs of hyrax droppings.

137

All antelope dung pellets fall into this group, although there is considerable variation in pellet size from species to species. It is crucial to take note of the way in which the pellets are deposited and the habitat in which you find them. Many species deposit their dung pellets in small heaps throughout their home range, others make use of latrine sites at all times, still others may use latrine sites only at certain times of the year. It is essential to check which species occur in the area where you are. For example, in the Kruger National Park you will not encounter signs left by Thomson's gazelle as this species is found only in parts of east Africa, nor will you find bongo signs outside the tropical forest belt.

There may be seasonal differences in the appearance of droppings, with animals eating lush, green plants having softer pellets that frequently adhere together. Pellets of animals that had consumed dry plant material are separate from each other. Droppings deposited in latrines may be of both types.

The key is meant as a *rough* guide to help you narrow down your identification of antelope pellets. We have selected those species of which the pellets are most frequently encountered and based the pellet sizes in the key on the average of 100 individual pellets from different deposits. Pellet size depends to some extent on the age of the animal and even on when droppings were deposited by the same animal. Lay the dung pellet on the key and once you have located a close fit, check your choice against the photographs and read the captions. You will notice that many of the photographs include everyday objects such as a matchstick (average length 42 mm) as an indication of size. We have done this deliberately as you are likely to have easy access to these items, whether out hiking or strolling.

Remember to note other signs that may help you, such as tracks and feeding signs, and the type of habitat. The outer surface of freshly dropped pellets is smooth and usually black or dark brown in colour.

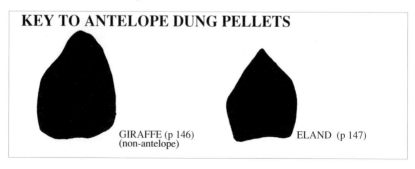

KEY TO ANTELOPE DUNG PELLETS

GIRAFFE (p 146)
(non-antelope)

ELAND (p 147)

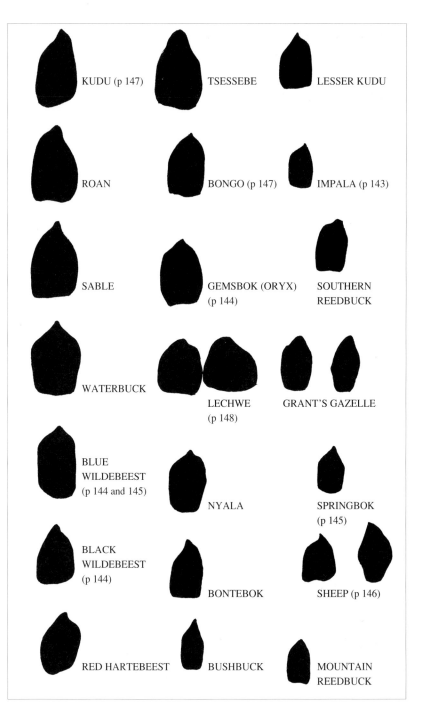

KUDU (p 147)

TSESSEBE

LESSER KUDU

ROAN

BONGO (p 147)

IMPALA (p 143)

SABLE

GEMSBOK (ORYX) (p 144)

SOUTHERN REEDBUCK

WATERBUCK

LECHWE (p 148)

GRANT'S GAZELLE

BLUE WILDEBEEST (p 144 and 145)

NYALA

SPRINGBOK (p 145)

BLACK WILDEBEEST (p 144)

BONTEBOK

SHEEP (p 146)

RED HARTEBEEST

BUSHBUCK

MOUNTAIN REEDBUCK

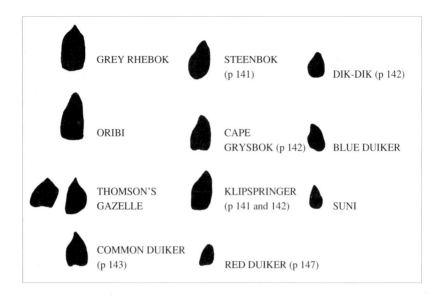

GREY RHEBOK

STEENBOK (p 141)

DIK-DIK (p 142)

ORIBI

CAPE GRYSBOK (p 142)

BLUE DUIKER

THOMSON'S GAZELLE

KLIPSPRINGER (p 141 and 142)

SUNI

COMMON DUIKER (p 143)

RED DUIKER (p 147)

A selection of antelope and giraffe dung pellets. Note that most have one pointed end, with the other end rounded, flat or slightly concave. Top row: giraffe, eland, greater kudu, black wildebeest; second row: gemsbok, blesbok, impala, bushbuck, mountain reedbuck; third row: Cape grysbok, Damara dik-dik; bottom row: oribi, klipspringer, common duiker, blue duiker, steenbok.

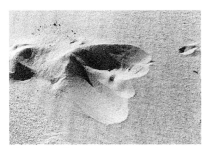

There is of course an exception to every rule: the steenbok is the only antelope that buries its droppings. The front hoofs are used to scratch a shallow depression into which the dung pellets and urine are dropped. These are then covered. A fresh site is used each time and most sites are located around the perimeter of the territory. The oribi, whose pellets look like those of the steenbok but are never buried, is an inhabitant of open grassland. It makes use of latrine sites but also deposits pellets (10-12 mm average) at random throughout its home range.

Exposed steenbok droppings. Individual pellets are usually 7-10 mm in length. This small antelope is widespread in southern and east Africa.

As already mentioned, a number of species deposit their droppings at regularly used latrine sites. Note that some other mammal species, particularly genets, the African civet and several mongooses, occasionally deposit their droppings on antelope latrines.

A large klipspringer latrine in a typical setting. These latrines are scattered throughout a family group's territory. They are usually on flat ground with a few isolated bushes in the mountainous or rugged, hilly terrain in which klipspringers live. Most are 1-1,5 m in diameter and several centimetres deep. Both sexes mark twigs

with a black, tarry substance secreted by the preorbital gland, and a search of twig tips near the latrines will reveal these marks. The darkest droppings are the most recent. This species is widely distributed in suitable habitat. Compare the photograph of a red rock rabbit latrine (page 149), as these latrines are found in similar locations to those of the klipspringer.

A small klipspringer latrine; note the small dried bush at bottom right, which had several glandular deposits on twig tips.

There are four species of dik-dik in east Africa and one in northern Namibia. Dik-dik family groups use communal latrines, which are not as obvious as those of other species because the rams scratch at the earlier deposits with the front hoofs, mixing the pellets with soil. The ewes do not dig before defecating. The dark pellets in this photograph were very fresh. Both sexes mark twigs and grass in the same way that klipspringers do.

The dung pellets of the Damara (Kirk's) dik-dik are usually in the 5-8 mm range.

Both Sharpe's and the Cape grysbok make use of communal latrines and mark twigs and grass stalks with pre-orbital gland secretions. Latrines may measure up to 1 m in diameter and reach depths of several centimetres. They are often in or close to fairly dense vegetation cover. This latrine, of a Cape grysbok, was located at the edge of a lucerne (alfalfa) field close to dense riverine scrub. Note the fresh, black pellets and older fused pellet clumps. Grysbok are found in the southern and south-western Cape Province, with other populations in the north-eastern part of southern Africa, extending into east Africa. Individual pellets average 10 mm in length.

142

The common (Grimm's) duiker is the most widespread of all duiker species and inhabits a range of bush habitats. It does not deposit its droppings at latrine sites in the way of the grysbok but individual piles frequently accumulate at favoured lying-up sites, giving the impression of latrines. These accumulations can become extensive and one site that we know covers approximately 60 m², with over 100 separate piles of droppings. Individual pellet deposits are also scattered throughout the territory. Most pellets are in the range of 10-12 mm. Note the individual pellets and the older clustered pellets in the photograph. Both sexes mark twigs with preorbital gland secretions.

A number of antelope species make use of seasonal latrine sites, but normally only the males do so. This type of latrine is usually clearly visible and considerable quantities of pellets may accumulate. These sites most often have a territorial function in association with the rut or breeding season.

A latrine created by an impala ram during the rut. Note the scattered heaps of pellets around the latrine. Impala pellets average 12-14 mm in length. Bachelor herds also tend to use latrine areas. Latrines are usually located in open ground near roads and pathways.

143

A latrine and rolling site used regularly by a gemsbok bull over a long period, as indicated by large quantities of old, pale pellets and the total absence of grass. This species occurs in the arid south-west, as well as in east Africa.

Fresh gemsbok droppings. Gemsbok, except bulls during the rut, drop pellets at random throughout the home range. Note the fresh tracks. Territorial bulls defecate in a low crouch which ensures that the pellets lie close together. In this way the scent is preserved for a longer period.

Although these gemsbok pellets retain their dark colouring, the cracking indicates that they are a few days old. Individual pellets are usually 14-20 mm long.

A blue wildebeest bull on its territorial "patch". Note that the area is bare of vegetation, and the scattering of droppings. The pellets are on average 20 mm in length.

The "patch" of a territorial blue wildebeest bull. Note the low harvester termite mounds; the termites make use of the dung pellets as well as the grass.

The black wildebeest bull also holds a territorial "patch". Note that the pellets are coagulated.

Clumped droppings of black wildebeest, an inhabitant of the grasslands of southern Africa.

An example of clumped pellets, in this case of springbok. The pellets were dropped only one minute before the photograph was taken. The location of the urine splash indicates that the animal was a female and its freshness is evidenced by the foam. There was an abundance of green plant food at this time, hence the softness of the pellets.

The following three photographs are of sheep droppings taken in different seasons. Pellets average 10 mm in length. Although these are typical examples you should always be aware that any of the forms can be present in any given season, and all may be present at the same time. This also applies to the antelope.

Early part of rainy season.

Well into the rains (note the dung beetle).

Dry season.

Okapi droppings: pellet average 23 mm. (Photo: Roland van Bocxstaele)

The largest dung pellets (average 30 mm) are those of the giraffe. Because of the height from which they fall they are usually more scattered than those of the eland and greater kudu.

146

The dung pellets of the eland are second in size (average 25 mm) only to those of the giraffe. This, the largest of all antelope, occurs widely in sub-Saharan Africa in savanna and semi-arid scrub.

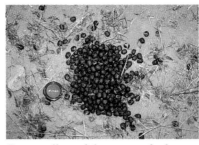

Dung pellets of the greater kudu usually measure 20 mm in length and are narrower than those of the eland and giraffe. In areas where greater kudu are common accumulations of pellets may be encountered in favoured feeding spots.

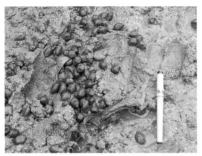

Bongo droppings: pellet average 22 mm. (Photo: Roland van Bocxstaele)

Like many duiker species, the red duiker usually defecates in specific areas, leaving small piles of dung close to each other. Note the pile of very fresh droppings and, to the side, the older droppings broken up by insects. Most duiker species inhabit forest and forest margins. The pellets of the red duiker average 8-10 mm in length and those of the very widespread blue duiker usually less than 8 mm. Latrine areas may be used by one or more individuals, and the latrines of many species have regularly used pathways radiating from them.

The red lechwe is an antelope of the wetlands and swamps of central Africa. As it consumes many water-rich plants the droppings are often misshapen but the usual pellet is 18 mm in length. Droppings are scattered at random throughout the home range.

Lozenge-shaped pellets in small scattered piles or large accumulations

This group includes the hares, rabbits and hyraxes. In the case of the hares and rabbits the individual pellets are spherical, firm and slightly flattened; they are lozenge-shaped like "Smarties". In cross-section they are oval and 10-15 mm in diameter. The hares, which occur widely in Africa, drop their pellets in small groups at random throughout the home range. The pellets do not have the dark coating of antelope droppings; they are mainly light in colour but dark pellets are occasionally found. The coarse plant material they contain is clearly visible.

The red rock rabbits (three species in southern and east Africa) deposit their droppings at large latrine sites, usually on flat rocks, which are more exposed than hyrax latrine sites. The pellets are easily distinguished from those of the klipspringer (see page 141 and 142). Pellets average 10 mm in diameter and when fresh are usually darker in colour than those of the hares. Red rock rabbits are found in mountainous and hilly country.

The dark, fresh pellets of a red rock rabbit. The pale grey pellets may be many months old.

The rock hyrax produces dung pellets similar to those of the red rock rabbits but they are more rounded and more variable. Single pellets or clusters are deposited at latrine sites close to the rock crevice homes of the hyraxes. Such accumulations can be very large. Hyrax species occur very widely; some occupy rocky habitats, others are tree-dwellers.

A characteristic of areas occupied by hyraxes is the streaking of white and dark brown deposits left by their urine.

The tree hyraxes or dassies (three species) have latrines located below shelter trees, or in tree hollows.

149

Grooved and ungrooved, flattened pellets

The dung pellets in this group superficially resemble flattened antelope pellets. They are found in small, scattered heaps and not in latrines. Many scattered heaps may be found at favoured feeding grounds.

The larger dung pellets of the greater canerat, and those of the vlei rat, which shares its reed and grass habitat. The canerat droppings have a groove on one surface (not shown in the photograph but see the key) and are usually associated with small piles of cut reeds and sedges on which this rodent feeds.
Individual pellets are about 20 mm in length and usually have a small point at one end. See also the feeding signs of these species on pages 200 and 203.

The dung pellets of a springhare and a Cape hare; both species are frequently found in the same habitat. Springhare pellets resemble those of the canerat but the species are separated by habitat. Springhares occupy open grassland in parts of southern and east Africa. Small heaps of pellets are scattered throughout the home range.

Droppings of mixed shape and form

This section comprises those droppings that vary in shape and form, or do not fit conveniently into the other categories. The group includes toad, earthworm, primate, porcupine, tortoise, bushpig, clawless otter and aardvark droppings.

The droppings of toads are all similar and are quite commonly found around houses, where they feed at night on insects attracted to lights. Size is variable but the droppings consist entirely of insect and other invertebrate parts. The fragments are clearly visible and the droppings crumble easily. They can be told from lizard droppings by the absence of a cap of white uric acid.

The droppings, or casts, of earthworms are commonly found in many areas, particularly when the soil is damp. Consisting entirely of soil, they are initially soft but soon harden. Size varies from a few to 35 mm in height, depending on the species. These were cast by one of the giant earthworms.

Chimpanzee droppings are scattered at random throughout the home range and contain mainly plant remains, although animal food is occasionally taken. You can see gorilla droppings in the photograph of a gorilla ground nest (page 239). The content is entirely plant remains.

Typical baboon dropping on a rock. The droppings of baboons are scattered at random throughout the home range but accumulations build up below roosts in large trees and on rocky outcrops. Shape and size vary greatly but fresh droppings have a thick porridge-like consistency and a relatively rough surface. They contain seeds and plant fragments and occasionally the remains of invertebrates. Baboons occur widely in the mountains and savannas of sub-Saharan Africa.

151

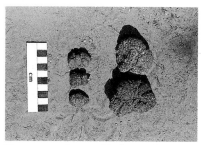

Vervet monkey and baboon drop-pings. The latter species also has a wide distribution in savanna areas. The droppings of most monkey species are similar but those of the colobus monkey contain mainly leaf fibres.

Vervet monkey droppings consist of plant fragments, particularly seeds and fruit skins, as in this case. Droppings are left at random.

Fresh porcupine droppings. They resemble date-stones or short, fat cigars in shape, usually 40-70 mm in length, and are dropped in clusters of up to 20 individual pellets which frequently adhere together. Droppings consist of coarse plant fibres. Those of animals that had fed on succulent bulbs may be mis-shapen. Droppings are randomly scattered throughout the home range, most notably along trails and on roads. The black-and-white banded quills are also commonly found. Porcupines have a wide habi-tat tolerance and occur throughout sub-Saharan Africa.

Tortoises produce droppings similar in shape to those of the porcupine but they are usually fatter and do not adhere together. The content is mostly coarse plant material as in these leopard tortoise droppings. Length varies from 20-100 mm, depending on the species.

152

Droppings of the bushpig usually have the shape of a blunt-ended sausage; they are up to 80 mm in diameter and made up of a series of oblong pellets. They are dropped at random along trails and at feeding sites. The bushpig occurs widely where there is adequate forest and woodland.

Bushpig droppings may be in one piece but they frequently fall apart.

Giant forest hog dung: this could be mistaken for that of the bushpig where they occur together, but is generally larger. Buffalo dung is similar but contains no individual pellets. The giant forest hog is restricted to dense tropical forest.

The droppings of the Cape clawless otter are often sausage-shaped but also come in other shapes, and they usually break up rapidly. They are dropped at latrine sites, nearly always close to rivers, lakes and dams. Crab remains make up the bulk of the content. The diameter of the average dropping is 22-30 mm. These are fresh droppings; note the older fragmented dropping on the right.

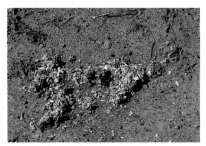

A broken-down otter dropping showing numerous crab fragments.

A typical otter latrine site.

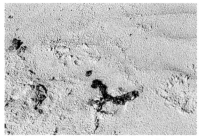

Otters use a small quantity of faeces, known as spraint, for marking in areas away from latrine sites, as shown here.

The aardvark produces compact pellets with no regular shape but made up mainly of soil and impregnated with the heads of termites. The droppings are buried, often at burrow entrances, so are rarely found. This unusual animal is found in most habitats except tropical forest and true desert.

Sausage-shaped droppings with a point at one end

This group includes the mongooses, genets, civets, members of the dog family, the spotted-necked otter and the hedgehogs. The dropping leaves the anus with the pointed end last. Some species deposit the droppings at latrine sites and others at random throughout the home range.

This selection of mongoose and striped weasel droppings indicates the size range. Clockwise from top left: water mongoose, yellow mongoose, dwarf mongoose, striped weasel, large grey mongoose, small grey mongoose.

A typical civetry.

The African civet deposits its droppings at latrines known as civetries. These are usually adjacent to roads or trails. Each civetry may be used by several animals. The folded remains of broad-leafed grass are commonly seen in the droppings of this animal, which may also include insect and other invertebrate fragments, hairs, feathers, small bones and seeds. The African civet marks rocks and tree stumps with a black anal gland secretion that has a distinct smell. This carnivore is widely distributed in tropical Africa. Note the folded bundles of broad-leafed grass in the droppings. (Photo: Peter Guy)

Although classed as a carnivore, the African civet frequently includes seeds and fruit in its diet. In this case the fruit of the wild date palm was eaten; the hard seeds passed undigested through the gut.

The latrine of a small-spotted genet at the edge of riverine woodland. As far as is known all genet species deposit their droppings at latrine sites, which may be located on rock ledges, at tree stumps, on the edge of clearings and even in the attics of buildings. The average diameter of droppings is 15 mm. They usually contain insect and other inverte-brate remains, feathers, hairs and occasionally seeds and grass.

An array of droppings taken from a single latrine site to show the varia-tion that can be expected in genets, in this case the small-spotted genet.

Yellow mongoose droppings. Both the yellow mongoose and the suri-cate are restricted to the central and western parts of southern Africa. Both species live in small warrens in relatively open areas. Their drop-pings are deposited in small latrines close to the warrens. In some areas they even share the same warrens. Both are mainly insect-eaters but sometimes the droppings of the yel-low mongoose contain large quanti-ties of millipede segments.

Fresh droppings of the yellow mon-goose (right) and the small, twisted droppings of the striped weasel. The latter are seldom found and are unlikely to be confused with the droppings of any other species.

The water (marsh) mongoose deposits its droppings at latrine sites on the ground, on grass clumps and on low shrubs near water. As the droppings break down they reveal large quantities of crab fragments, as well as insect remains, hairs, feathers and small bones. This photograph shows a latrine on open ground on a riverbank.

A water mongoose latrine among dead branches on the ground. Most droppings are about 20 mm in diameter. The droppings of the Cape clawless otter are much larger (up to 30 mm in diameter) and the latrines are more extensive; the droppings of the spotted-necked otter average 15 mm in diameter, are also deposited in latrines and are made up mainly of crab and fish remains. The scent of fresh otter droppings is usually fishy but that of the water mongoose is not.

A typical spotted-necked otter dropping. (Photo: Dave Rowe-Rowe)

A small deposit of dwarf mongoose droppings (average diameter 8 mm). These animals live in small troops and take shelter in such sites as the ventilation shafts of large termite mounds. Each troop may make use of several such shelters. They deposit their droppings in small latrines close to their shelters. The larger banded mongoose also lives in troops, uses similar shelters and makes use of latrine sites, but the droppings are about twice as large (average diameter 12-16 mm). Both species feed mainly on insects and invertebrates and occur widely in tropical Africa.

157

The droppings of members of the dog family are similar but vary in size and in some cases in content. Those of the wild dog, now one of Africa's rarest mammals, are usually dark in colour and are frequently eaten by such species as the spotted hyaena and black-backed jackal.

The fresh dropping of a bat-eared fox. These animals live in small family parties and make use of communal latrine sites, often near maternity dens but also at other places throughout the home range. The average diameter of the droppings is 18 mm. Droppings contain mainly insect fragments, but when edible berries are available they may contain large quantities of seeds and fruit skins. There are two separate bat-eared fox populations, one in east and one in southern Africa. This is mainly a species of savanna habitats.

The black-backed jackal is common in many areas of southern and east Africa. It has the useful habit of depositing its droppings in prominent places, such as on grass clumps, small shrubs and rocks, usually along trails and roads. This jackal does not make use of latrines but small accumulations, as in this photograph, may be encountered. The dark dropping is fresh, the white ones are older. Some droppings may have a slightly segmented appearance and could be confused with those of the caracal. The black-backed jackal eats a very wide range of food.

This is the result of a black-backed jackal having a bout of diarrhoea; be aware that not all droppings will be as you expect.

The droppings of the southern African hedgehog.

Sausage-shaped droppings, tapered at one end and usually segmented

Droppings in this group are deposited by the hyaenas, the aardwolf and the cats. The spotted and brown hyaenas have the useful habit of depositing their large white droppings at prominent latrine sites. The whiteness of the droppings is as a result of the animals' consuming considerable quantities of bone fragments. Although the spotted hyaena occurs widely in Africa, the brown hyaena is restricted to the drier areas of southern Africa. A third species, the striped hyaena of northern and north-eastern Africa, also deposits its dung at latrine sites.

A typical spotted hyaena latrine site: the droppings are fairly dispersed and may sometimes cover several hundred square metres. Latrines may be in the centre or on the edges of a clan's territory, depending on the region. Where roads pass through a territory the animals frequently create latrine sites near them. Some latrines may have numerous droppings, others only a few. The droppings of this species are up to three times larger (150 g) than those of the brown hyaena (about 50 g).

159

By contrast the latrine of the brown hyaena has the droppings much closer together and is nearly always in a slight depression. Like those of the spotted hyaena, latrines may be located next to roads; they are scattered throughout the territory, mostly near the boundary, but we have located latrines close to den sites. Note the concentration of droppings, the small, dark fresh deposit and the wet urine patch.

Fresh hyaena droppings are greenish in colour. These are of a brown hyaena; note the seeds of the tsamma melon. The spotted hyaena rarely eats any plant food. Be aware that the droppings of lion, leopard and cheetah may also turn white; they are however not deposited at latrine sites but at random.

Hyaena droppings soon dry and whiten as a result of the high bone content of the animal's diet.

The small, hyaena-like aardwolf, which occurs in separate populations in southern and east Africa, produces very large droppings for its size. Aardwolf defecate in latrines, with up to 20 such sites in each territory, each measuring 1-2 m in diameter. A narrow trench is excavated with the front paws, into which the animal defecates and usually also urinates. The hole may be partly closed but droppings are always visible on the surface. The aardwolf eats almost exclusively termites and its droppings contain large quantities of soil and numerous termite heads.

All of the cats produce droppings that are similar in overall appearance but of course vary in size. Only the African wild cat deposits droppings at latrine sites. However, loose accumulations of other cat droppings may be encountered at lying-up sites, near a large kill or, in the case of the leopard, at trail crossings, but these droppings rarely number more than a few. We have encountered small accumulations at the dens of females with cubs.

Fresh lion droppings; note the segmentation. Droppings made up mainly of digested blood and flesh retain a dark colour but those containing much calcium from bones whiten when they dry. Although the droppings look like those of hyaenas, they are scattered at random. The diameter is usually more than 40 mm, but be aware that there is much variation. Lions occur widely in Africa but are mainly restricted to conservation areas.

A lion dropping with a high calcium content.

An example of a soft lion dropping without segmentation.

Three examples of leopard droppings collected over a distance of 2 km along the same trail. As you can see, size varies. Note the segmentation and the colour. The leopard, like all cats, makes frequent use of roads and trails to avoid "bush bashing" when moving around its territory. Droppings and tracks are fairly easy to see on these trails. The diameter of droppings of leopards in the Cape coastal mountains of South Africa range from 20-30 mm; those elsewhere are usually larger but never as large as droppings produced by adult lion. See also the photograph of caracal droppings .

A weathered leopard dropping clearly showing the hoof and hair of a klipspringer.

Typical caracal (left) and leopard droppings collected in the southern Cape Province, South Africa. Caracal droppings rarely have a diameter exceeding 20 mm. This cat has a wide habitat tolerance and is absent only from tropical forest. Like those of all cats the droppings usually contain large quantities of hair.

Fresh cheetah droppings; note the position of the tracks and that the clear print of the main pads shows the double indentation on the trailing edges, but hardly any claw marks.The diameter of cheetah droppings is 25-35 mm.

Cheetah droppings. The use by cheetah of specific trees in which they "play" has been recorded only in Namibia, but several droppings may be found in the vicinity of these trees, including on sloping branch surfaces. There is also a strong smell of urine and numerous tracks are present around trees in regular use. These trees are well known to stock and game farmers who set traps to catch cheetah at these locations.

The African wild cat may bury its droppings, as seen here, at random throughout its territory in much the same way as the domestic cat, but it also deposits droppings in latrines. In our experience the latrines are located close to the den or lying-up site. The diameter of the droppings usually ranges from 12-15 mm.

The same African wild cat scrape with the droppings exposed.

Three other cat species occur in sub-Saharan Africa, the golden cat, serval and small-spotted cat. We have no information on the droppings of the golden cat, which inhabits the tropical forest zone. The droppings of the serval are similar to those of the caracal but on average slightly smaller. The serval is a medium-sized cat which inhabits mainly grassland, reedbeds and forest fringes; the droppings are made up largely of rodent hair and bone fragments. The droppings of captive small-spotted cats have a range of 10-14 mm in diameter. We have never found proven small-spotted cat droppings in the field.

Kidney-shaped droppings

This form of dropping is produced by the horse, donkey and the zebra species. We have also included the widespread warthog here as its droppings bear a superficial resemblance to those of the horse family.

Droppings of the horse family have a distinct kidney shape and each pellet usually develops a crack across the centre. Usually 10 to 30 separate pellets are dropped at a time. When fresh they are light to dark brown in colour but usually dry to almost black. The zebras deposit their droppings at random throughout the home range. All species are grazers and are associated with grassland of various types. The plains zebra is widespread in central and east Africa, as well as in the eastern and northern parts of southern Africa. Hartmann's zebra is mainly restricted to western Namibia. The rare Cape mountain zebra is found in a few conservation areas in southern South Africa. Grevy's zebra has a limited distribution in Kenya and the horn of Africa.

Fresh horse droppings.

Horse and zebra droppings are frequently broken up by birds, such as francolins, searching for grass seed and insects.

Plains zebra droppings average 50 mm in length. During the dry season pellets may retain their form for several months if not broken up by birds.

Droppings of Grevy's zebra; the track in the foreground is of a beisa oryx. Grevy's zebra and the plains zebra may be found in loose association in northern Kenya. It is not possible to separate their droppings. Territorial Grevy's zebra stallions deposit their droppings in piles to mark their territories; plains zebra stallions do not do this.

Warthog droppings, although similar to those of the zebras, are usually dropped in smaller numbers, are less than 50 mm in length and do not crack across the middle. No latrine sites are used.

Thick "pancake-like" droppings

Most people are familiar with the semi-liquid, roughly circular piles of faeces (cow-pats) produced by cattle, as well as by buffalo. During the dry season, or when animals are eating dry plant material, the droppings are firmer and more layered. Cattle and buffalo occur widely in Africa.

Buffalo dung.

Cattle dung.

Always watch out for "variations on a theme". These are the droppings of an eland that had been feeding on plant food with a high water content. A quick glance would have passed them off as cow-pats or buffalo dung, but closer examination clearly shows the form of the individual pellets.

165

Large, barrel-shaped droppings

This group comprises the droppings of the heavyweights: the elephant, the rhinoceros species and the hippopotamus. The intact droppings of these species superficially resemble squat barrels of the type used to mature liquor: slightly bulging at the centre and flat at both ends.

Elephants deposit their droppings at random but large quantities may accumulate at water points and at favoured feeding sites. When fresh the droppings may have a greenish to yellow colour, depending on the type of food taken, but as they dry they may darken, particularly if they dry in the shade. Individual droppings may be 20 cm or more in length but those of young animals are obviously smaller. They contain coarse plant fibres, leaves and seeds. An adult elephant may produce as much as 100 kg of dung in 24 hours.

Elephants may deposit soft droppings when under stress, or if their food has a high water content.

A very useful aid to identifying the rhinoceros species is the content of the droppings. The white rhino is a grazer and the content of the dung is fairly uniform in appearance, with relatively fine plant fibres.

The black rhino is a browser and the dung consists of woody, coarse plant material mixed with finer material.

Both rhinoceros species make use of latrine sites, although they may also defecate at random within the home range; the differences are individual and sexual. After depositing the dung the bulls of both species kick it vigorously with the hind feet. The black rhino leaves distinct parallel scrape marks while doing this: they are clearly seen in this photograph. Note how the droppings are broken up. Fresh droppings of both species are dark green but they soon darken as they dry. In southern African conservation areas where both rhinos occur together, latrine sites may be shared. Both rhinoceros species are now mainly restricted to conservation areas in southern Africa, with very small numbers in east Africa.

Black rhino latrine at the side of a road.

A latrine used by a white rhino bull; note the completely fragmented dung.

The hippo produces droppings similar to those of the elephant and the two rhinos but averaging only 10 cm in length. Droppings can be found throughout the grazing grounds but the most characteristic sign is the accumulations of broken-up dung clinging to bushes. Bulls turn their ample posteriors towards these marking sites and as the droppings are expelled the short fat tail is flicked rapidly from side to side, causing the dung to be broken up and scattered. These marking sites are most abundant close to water. Hippos are widespread in tropical Africa.

Hippo droppings.

168

Liquid droppings

The origins of liquid "splash" droppings, with or without additional material, are difficult and often impossible to determine. Nearly all are produced by birds but there are a couple of exceptions, namely fruit bats that have eaten very soft fruits, and hyraxes, whose urine stains on cliffs can easily be mistaken for the droppings of colonially roosting and nesting birds such as the Cape griffon and the bald ibis. The hyrax rarely makes use of very high, vertical cliffs but may shelter near the top or bottom of such sites. The droppings of fruit bats (colour may range from yellowish to purple) are most clearly seen splashed on the walls of buildings, much to the annoyance of the owners.

Certain colonial tree-nesting birds, such as the whitebreasted cormorant, darter, reed cormorant and some herons, produce very acid droppings which may eventually kill the trees and surrounding vegetation.

Faecal streaks at the roost of a rock kestrel. The raptors (birds of prey) are able to squirt their faeces over considerable distances.

169

Urine streaks at a hyrax colony. Colonial cliff-roosting birds usually occupy much higher cliffs than those used by the hyrax.

Many birds sit on prominent perches within their territory and have no inhibitions about soiling their vantage points.

The droppings of birds of prey are very liquid and are usually sprayed over an impressive area. This is the work of a steppe buzzard.

A telephone pole used as a daytime perch by a jackal buzzard; note the distance that the droppings were sprayed onto the road!

The ostrich, befitting its prodigious size, excretes a large amount of faecal matter at a time. The droppings always have a liquid and a semi-solid component. This bird is frequently encountered.

Three examples of typical ostrich droppings.

The droppings of a redwinged starling on damp ground. Note the dark liquid component and the seeds that have passed undamaged through the gut. We saw these droppings being deposited, hence the identification, but in general it is not possible to identify species from liquid droppings.

Formed sausage, usually dry and firm, with partial white coating

Gamebirds such as francolins, guineafowl, bustards, pigeons and waterfowl produce droppings of this kind. The shape may vary according to season and diet. Droppings are deposited at random where the birds move about but may accumulate at roosts. Coarse plant fibres are usually clearly visible.

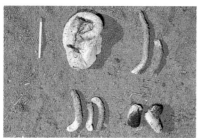 

Examples of the type of droppings in this group, clockwise from top left: Ludwig's bustard, helmeted guineafowl, rock pigeon (wet season), Swainson's francolin.

Ludwig's bustard droppings collected in the wet season. Members of the bustard family occur throughout Africa, except in the tropical forest belt.

Droppings of Swainson's francolin. The droppings of the many francolin species are similar in appearance; in the rainy season they tend to be rounder and darker. Large quantities of droppings may accumulate at favoured roosts.

Accumulated droppings below a hel-
meted guineafowl tree-roost. Note
the feather, an aid to identification.

Droppings below a rock pigeon
roost in a rock overhang. This
species is commonly associated with
buildings as well. Note the tight,
coiled spring appearance which is
typical of pigeon and dove drop-
pings.

Goose and duck droppings are simi-
lar to those of the gamebirds but
tend to be softer when fresh. They
are often dark green in colour,
although fading with age. Large
quantities may accumulate at water
bodies. These are the droppings of
the widespread Egyptian goose.

**Formed sausage, usually pointed at both ends, with a hard cap of
white or yellowish uric acid**

Snakes and lizards produce droppings of this kind but with a few exceptions
they are seldom located and it is seldom possible to identify the species
involved. We have only rarely encountered snake droppings but in rock
crevices, stone walls, tree-hole entrances and buildings you may find lizard
droppings. At sun-basking and resting sites small accumulations may build
up but droppings are generally scattered at random. Size varies from a few

173

millimetres to 10 cm, depending on the species involved. Most species eat insects but some are specialist feeders, such as certain agamas which eat mainly ants.

Droppings of the flap-necked chameleon.

Bibron's gecko droppings: our identification is positive because the depositor lives in our bathroom.

Bird pellets

Birds, unlike mammals, do not chew their food but swallow it whole, or tear it into pieces small enough to swallow. Although it is commonly known that the raptors produce pellets which are regurgitated, it is seldom realised that many other bird species also get rid of inedible food remains in this way. These birds include the herons, crows, gulls, storks, bee-eaters, kingfishers, shrikes, some starlings and the dikkops.

The narrow pyloric opening (an extension of the stomach) of birds allows the passage of only small food items, and the absence of free acidity in the stomach prevents complete digestion. Stomach acidity is particularly weak in the owls. Consequently undigested food remains, such as feathers, hair, bones and invertebrate fragments, and this is periodically regurgitated in the form of pellets. Hard parts of the food items are usually enclosed in softer material such as hair, feathers and vegetable fibres. Each pellet has a coating of mucus when fresh.

It is possible in some cases to identify the species of bird by its regurgitated pellets. The pellets of the owls are particularly valuable for scientific study because prey is swallowed whole and the pellets often contain small mammal skulls and bones. Not only is it possible to determine the diet of a species but pellets also provide a rapid indication of the presence and relative abundance of small mammals and other animals in an area.

Pellets are scattered at random throughout a bird's home range but may accumulate at roosts and nesting sites. To identify the bird responsible for a pellet one has to consult distribution maps and look at the habitat and the pellet contents. In general, the larger the bird, the larger the pellet, but there is considerable variation within any one species and there are no standard

174

pellet sizes. For example, most owls produce larger pellets at their daytime roosts than at hunting perches. The following photographs illustrate the bird pellets that we have most frequently encountered.

Regurgitated bird pellets. Top row: crowned eagle, tawny eagle, grey heron, cattle egret; middle: greater kestrel, steppe buzzard; bottom row: barn owl, grass owl, kelp gull, black crow.

The pellets of the very widespread barn owl are frequently encountered, partly because these owls often roost and breed in buildings, but also because of the large numbers of pellets that accumulate. They also make use of holes in cliffs and tree hollows. Here many pellets had fallen to the ground below a roost located in a shallow rock hollow. The pellets  *when fresh have a black, glossy appearance which is retained if they are dropped under cover. Roosts are often in use for many years and as the older pellets break down the small bones and skulls they contained litter the surrounding area, as in this photograph.*

Typical barn owl pellets; note the coating of hair and dried mucus that encloses the sharp bones. The pellets are roughly oval in shape and average 50 mm in length. Small mammal, bird and lizard skulls in the pellets of this species are usually undamaged but those found in the pellets of the eagle owls are usually crushed.

Occasionally you will encounter pellets that are atypical, such as these barn owl pellets. The three on the left contain the legs and feathers of small waders taken by the owl on coastal mud-flats. An awkward meal!

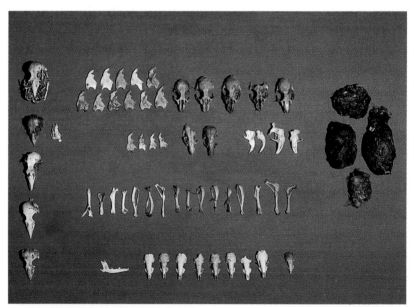

A selection of skulls, mandibles and other bones removed from barn owl pellets. Vertical row at left: bird skulls; top row: jaws and skulls of vlei rats (Otomys spp.); second row: striped mouse jaws and skulls, common molerat, whole pellets; third row: rodent and shrew bones; bottom row: jaw of elephant shrew, skulls of two shrew species.

176

Pellets of a whitefaced owl. This species feeds mainly on small rodents but birds are occasionally taken.

The vultures also regurgitate pellets which usually consist of hair and items such as hoofs. Other material is usually broken down by efficient digestive acids. The two smaller pellets are those of a whitebacked vulture, the larger pellet that of a lappetfaced vulture. We emphasise that there is no standard pellet size; although most lappetfaced vulture pellets are large we have seen several of under 60 mm in length.

A lappetfaced vulture pellet with antelope hair and hoofs.

Pellets of the blackheaded and the grey heron are very similar. They are most frequently encountered at nesting and roosting colonies. These herons eat a wide range of food, including rodents, reptiles, birds, insects and other invertebrates. Pellet shape is variable but often roughly circular.

Cattle egret pellets usually contain mostly insect and other animal remains but we have also found large quantities of seed, as in these pellets.

Pied crow (also black crow) pellets contain much plant material, as well as a wide range of animal remains. The best place to look for crow pellets is at roost sites – usually tall trees – but also check below telephone posts where these birds commonly nest.

Kelp gull pellets; note the piece of plastic in the larger pellet. These birds scavenge and almost anything can be expected in their pellets.

Pellets regurgitated by small birds are rarely found as they are scattered at random and usually break down rapidly. This pellet was produced by a fiscal shrike.

5 FEEDING SIGNS

All living animals must feed in order to sustain life and during their foraging they leave signs that can assist you in determining the species involved. The number of feeding places is largely dependent on the type of food that an animal eats and the way in which it collects, hunts or scavenges the food. For example, the food of carnivores has a high nutritional value and therefore the individual requires only a small quantity to sustain itself. On the other hand herbivores eat food of low nutritional value and therefore they must eat frequently, and large amounts. This increases the number of feeding locations. Species that forage for insects usually excavate numerous shallow holes and in this way leave signs that are easily observed.

Some feeding signs may remain visible for long periods, for example a tree pushed over by an elephant to gain access to pods, but a lion kill may be reduced to a few large bones in a matter of hours by spotted hyaenas, black-backed jackals and vultures. Feeding signs may include claw and tooth marks, holes in trees or in the ground, remains of prey, damaged fruit and other plant parts.

Also look around for other signs that may give you additional clues, such as tracks and droppings. From the tracks try to determine whether you are looking at the feeding signs left by one individual, or a herd, as this will also help your identification. You should aim at building up as complete a picture as possible and you may well find, as we have, that doing so provides as much excitement and interest as seeing the animal itself. By following fresh elephant tracks we were once able to identify more than 20 plant species eaten by a herd over a distance of less than 2 km. We could clearly see the place where palms were shaken to dislodge the fruit, balls of chewed palm leaf fibres that the animals had discarded, an acacia tree pushed over to gain access to the tender growth tips and small quantities of grass pulled out by the roots.

By following a set of caracal tracks we were able to find the place where it had crouched and then lunged at a covey of Cape francolin. There were a few feathers but all the birds had escaped. Some 500 m further the caracal had succeeded in catching a scrub hare and here it was joined by a second cat. This puzzled us but a few metres further we found tracks indicating that the animals had mated. So we were able not only to gain some knowledge of diet and hunting technique but also to record mating. All this without ever catching a glimpse of the animals!

We have selected photographs of feeding signs to aid you in identifying the species involved but remember that these are only a few of the possibilities. However, they include those signs that you are most likely to encounter. With some detective work and careful observation you may well find that you are able to reach an identification.

Evidence of predation by mammals and birds is normally only encountered if the prey had been large; small prey items rarely leave any sign. Always be careful not to jump to conclusions when examining remains: the animal may have already been dead and merely scavenged, not killed; even if it had been killed the tracks you find could be of scavengers that fed after the killer had eaten its fill; on hot days a carcass will decompose rapidly and identifying signs could be lost. Find out which predators and raptors occur in the area, compare the signs and habits of the different species and examine the surrounding area in great detail. Lions kill and eat a surprising variety of prey species, from young elephants to porcupines. To kill their prey lions may aim the bite at one of several places, depending on the size of the animal being taken. Large mammals are usually taken by the throat whereas smaller mammals, with weaker bones, are usually bitten on the nape. Another method frequently used by lions is to grasp the prey by the snout, thereby suffocating it. Large prey animals frequently have lacerations on the rump and shoulders. Lions may stay in the vicinity of a large kill and eat over a period of several days, but they just as frequently move away and do not return. Lions will eat the skin, muscle tissue, some bones and the viscera, but the contents of the stomach and intestines are discarded and often buried. Once the lions move off, the scavengers move in and a carcass can be dismembered and stripped in a very short time.

This eland cow was killed by a pride of lions and further eaten by spotted hyaenas and black-backed jackals. The absence of vulture droppings indicates that the prey was killed at night and little remained to attract them.

The neck of this impala ewe was broken; the kill was adjacent to a dense reedbed.

The leopard takes a much wider array of prey items than the lion. Large animals are usually dispatched with a nape or throat bite. If you skin the neck of a kill you should be able to locate the puncture marks made by the canine teeth: the upper canines average 45 mm apart and the lower canines 35 mm. The neck of large prey is often broken. After making a kill, a leopard drags or carries the carcasss to cover, often leaving a distinct drag mark if the prey is fairly large. Drag distances may be a few metres but up to 2 km. Leopards frequently return to a kill, which they either hide by covering it with vegetation, or lodge in a tree. Small prey is usually entirely consumed. Muscle tissue of large prey is usually eaten from the buttock region and the shoulder and internal organs may be consumed, but the stomach and intestines are discarded and often buried under debris. Long bones of large prey are not broken as in spotted hyaena and lion kills.

Cheetah, which feed mainly on medium-sized antelope, kill their prey almost exclusively by strangulation: the animal is held by the throat until it dies. The skin is usually punctured, but only slightly, and haemorrhaging is light. The upper canines average 35 mm apart, the lower incisors being slightly closer together. Cheetah usually start eating from the rump, abdomen and rib cage, then the shoulders, the liver and heart. Large bones are not broken. Prey is usually dragged to cover.

Always be aware of possible varia-
tions in eating method; this sheep
had been killed by a small leopard
that had fed only on the meat around
the backbone. Leopards may kill
more sheep or goats than they need
and carry away just one on which to
feed. This rarely happens with wild
prey species.

The front leg and shoulder of this
sheep were torn off by a leopard – a
clear indication of this cat's great
strength.

The caracal, a medium-sized cat of over 8 kg, takes mainly mammal prey up
to the size of bushbuck ewes. Larger prey, in our experience, is usually killed
with a throat bite but the caracal will also use a nape bite. The upper
canines average 29 mm apart and the lower canines 23 mm. The bite marks
show as two small punctures on either side of the windpipe or on either side
of the spine. Claw marks may be present on the shoulder, belly or rump. The
caracal in the photograph is executing a throat bite. Note how the front paw
holds the animal down.

A grey rhebok ewe killed by a caracal. This cat typically feeds on the flesh between the hind legs or on the inside of a hind leg; it will also feed on the brisket and the shoulders. Although rib tips may be chewed, large bones are never eaten. Prey is only rarely removed from the kill site. (Photo: Dave Rowe-Rowe)

Flesh removed by a caracal from the inside of one hind leg of a grey rhebok.

A bushbuck ewe killed with a throat bite by a caracal; note the typical way in which flesh has been eaten from the inside of the hind legs. (Photo: Tommy Heinecken)

A steenbok killed by a caracal; note how the flesh has been eaten from the inside of the hind legs.

This bushbuck was killed by a caracal but later dismembered by a bushpig. The bushpig will readily feed from carcasses and the bones may become spread over quite a large area.

183

The black-backed jackal is an opportunistic feeder, taking anything from berries, insects, rodents and mammals up to the size of small antelope to the young of sheep and goats, such as this lamb. We use photographs of domestic stock kills here to illustrate certain characteristics but please don't think they form an important part of the jackal's diet: they do not. At larger kills look for two small puncture marks on either side of the windpipe (upper canines 25 mm apart, lower canines 22 mm apart), or for marks left by the upper canines under the eye and behind the ear, with the lower canine marks on the oesophagus and arteries.

A goat kid killed and eaten by a black-backed jackal. Jackals do not remove larger prey from the kill site. The carcass is usually opened on the flank between the hip and the bottom of the ribs. The skin may be neatly peeled back and the internal organs eaten (the gut may be discarded but we have seen cases where it has been eaten); flesh over the rib cage and other meat may also be consumed. In the case of lambs, goat kids and the young of small antelope only the head, legs and skin may be left.

184

A lamb killed and partly eaten by a black-backed jackal. The Cape fox (south-ern Africa only) may occasionally take young lambs. It bites in the lower part of the back and at the back of the neck. Tooth marks are very small (upper canines 16 mm apart, lower canines 14 mm apart). The Cape fox first opens the belly and the viscera are eaten; if more than one fox is involved they also eat a small portion of the buttock muscle. This fox frequently returns to a kill but no attempt is made to move the prey from the kill site.

A common duiker killed by a black-backed jackal; note how the skin has been peeled back from the ribs.

A young steenbok killed by a black-backed jackal; note that the skin is peeled back and flesh-free. Pied crows also fed on the carcass.

185

Domestic dogs are responsible for many attacks on sheep and goats, particularly on the commercial farms of southern Africa. These photographs illustrate the type of injuries that result from dog attacks. Bites can be located anywhere on the body of the victim and more than one animal is usually killed or maimed. In many cases nothing is eaten but occasionally the carcass may be ripped open and partly eaten. (Photos: John Carlyon)

The large eagles, such as the black (Verreaux's), tawny, martial and crowned, capture relatively large prey. This steenbok was killed by a black eagle and the bird fed on the muscle tissue of the shoulder. Puncture marks from the powerful talons may be located along the back, neck or head of larger prey. The powerful beak tears the flesh; large bones are never removed but deep wedge-shaped marks made by the beak may be seen on the outer edge of the scapula (shoulder blade). (Photo: André Boshoff)

This sheep had been killed and partly eaten by a caracal but a jackal buzzard then fed on the shoulder region (note the beak marks in the scapula) and pied crows stripped the face of eyes and flesh. Look for white droppings of birds at carcasses.

This lamb died of natural causes but pied crows pecked out the eyes very soon after death, as can be seen from the blood on the facial wool. The absence of bite marks on the carcass and signs of a struggle indicated that no predator was involved.

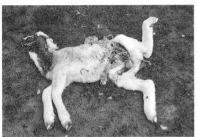

The same lamb four hours later. The pied crows had returned and were then chased off by a small grey mongoose. At our approach the rotund mongoose ran off into cover. That night a water mongoose ate a considerable amount. An inexperienced person could well have presumed that one of the mongooses, or the crows, killed the lamb.

A helmeted guineafowl killed and partly eaten by a Wahlberg's eagle. Note the eagle's tracks in the foreground and to the left of the prey, the dropping in the background and the plucked feathers. This raptor does not pluck clean.

Baboons are predominantly vegetarian but they do take animal food when it is available. This hyrax was caught by a baboon, which ate everything except the peeled-back skin and the front part of the skull. There are no characteristic features at baboon prey remains so look for tracks and droppings in the close vicinity.

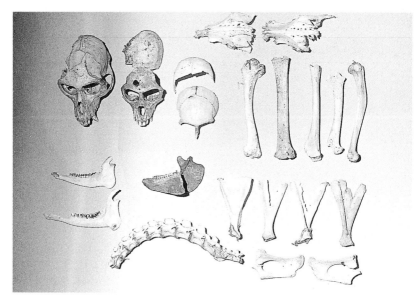

Prey remains collected below the nest of a pair of crowned eagles. Top right: pelvises of large birds (hadedas?); first row left to right: vervet monkey skulls, various leg bones; second row: jaw of blue duiker with jaw of Cape grysbok below it, jaw of tree hyrax, antelope scapulae (note the V-shaped tears in their broader edges); bottom row: mammal vertebrae, antelope pelvises.

The scapula of a blue duiker with a puncture made by the talon of a crowned eagle and beak marks along the soft edge. A number of raptors leave these characteristic beak marks on the scapulae of mammals and the sternums of birds.

The cranium of a vervet monkey opened by the talons and beak of a crowned eagle. This gives an indication of the power of these birds.

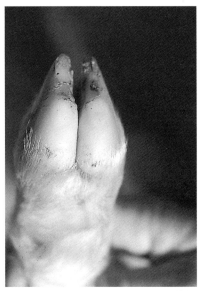

Many animals die of disease or injuries, and what may initially seem to be a kill may in fact be an animal that had died of other causes. These vultures and the marabou storks are feeding on a blue wildebeest that had died of disease.

The underside of the hoof of a still-born lamb. Note that there are no rough edges and the surface is completely smooth; the hoofs of a lamb that had walked would show rough edges and surface scuffing. This is a sure way of assessing whether a young ungulate had walked after birth.

This blue wildebeest cow had died of starvation during a severe drought and was stripped of flesh and viscera by vultures. An unusual scavenger, this warthog fed on the gut content as well as the flesh of the wildebeest. This is not typical behaviour but goes to emphasise the need to be always aware that things do not necessarily follow a set pattern. Bushpig will readily scavenge from carcasses but it is rare for warthog to do so.

189

The remains of a young gemsbok killed by cheetah; when they had had their fill these black-backed jackals moved in. Within a few hours the only evidence of such a kill is a scattering of bones and some skin, much of which will be carried away by hyaenas. (Photo: John Carlyon)

The remains of a red lechwe killed by poachers and within a couple of hours picked clean by vultures. If poachers have to travel long distances they usually remove only those pieces with the most flesh, such as the hind legs and shoulders. Examine bones for machete (panga) marks and severe damage to bones that could have resulted from bullet wounds.

Large numbers of animals die on fences: antelope when trying to jump over them, and smaller species that get caught in netting. Most of these casualties attract scavengers. This Cape hare tried to pass through a hole in wire netting but got stuck. Crows ate from it while it was still alive: this could be determined from the blood that was spattered on the ground and smeared on the face after the eyes had been pecked out. If the hare had been dead there would have been no blood spatters.

The Cape clawless otter feeds mainly on crabs, frogs, small mammals, freshwater mussels and occasionally fish, but at times it may attack domestic poultry, such as these ducks. They had been placed in a pen for the night and it was easy for the otter to kill several birds, something rarely possible in the wild. They were all bitten around the neck, some had legs ripped off and some breast meat was eaten.

The remains of a white (European) stork that had been killed by a cheetah. There was fresh blood on some feathers and on the ground at the kill site 120 m away. Predator identification was based on the tracks at the kill site and droppings at the feeding location. Cheetah readily take birds up to the size of an ostrich.

Many birds of prey hunt and feed on birds. The falcons do not pluck prey as thoroughly as the accipiters (for example goshawks and sparrowhawks) and they tear V-shaped pieces out of the sternum (breastbone). The accipiters do not damage the sternum but clean it thoroughly of flesh. The intestines and stomach are carefully removed and discarded. Both groups of raptor make use of "butchers" or plucking blocks which may be in a tree, on the ground or on a rock. They may have favoured plucking blocks, particularly during the breeding season. This pale chanting goshawk is feeding on a dove it had caught at a waterhole. Feathers may blow over considerable distances.

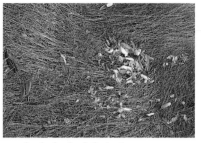

Two examples of sites where lanner falcons had plucked their dove prey. Many of the smaller raptors will cache prey items in times of abundance; these may be neatly lined up on a branch, rock or vacant nest. We have encountered the headless carcasses of several quail that had been set in line by a rednecked falcon on the edge of an old lappetfaced vulture nest.

Hereby a tale! A Namaqua sandgrouse female was sitting on three eggs when a blackbreasted snake eagle stooped and snatched her from the nest, in the process breaking only one of the eggs. The raptor started to feed on the sandgrouse but we disturbed it and it flew off with the bird in its talons. Even if we had not observed the kill it would still have been possible to identify it as having been the work of a raptor from the plucked feathers, the fresh faecal splash and the fact that although one egg was broken no attempt had been made to eat them. A mammalian predator would almost certainly have eaten the eggs.

A Cape cormorant carcass that was scavenged by kelp gulls: there were no blood spots on the damp sand, which indicates that it was dead before the gulls started feeding; the tracks clearly showed which species of gull was involved.

Some scavengers, such as the black-backed jackal, cache food at distinctive midden sites. This behaviour is particularly prevalent on the west coast of southern Africa. The brown hyaena also holds caches but usually close to den sites. Bones are accumulated by porcupines and these are most frequently encountered in rocky overhangs and shallow caves. Bones collected by this species usually have distinctive gnaw marks.

A barbel caught and eaten by a fish eagle. These eagles usually carry small fish to tree perches but large specimens are carried to the river or lake bank. Note the discarded glands in the foreground, the long faecal squirt (a sure sign of raptor) and the large quantities of meat that have been eaten. Such remains are usually very quickly eaten or removed by scavengers. At favoured feeding trees and nest sites large quantities of fish bones and skulls accumulate.

The water mongoose eats large quantities of crabs but unlike otters does not completely consume the crabs. One usually finds the discarded carapace, pincers and legs of larger specimens lying at the water's edge.

The Cape clawless otter will eat large quantities of freshwater mussels where these occur and substantial numbers of smashed shells accumulate at regularly used "anvil sites". The otter holds the whole shell in the front paws while hammering it against the "anvil" and also throws larger specimens in order to smash them. The water mongoose also smashes mussels but one never sees large accumulations of shells as is the case with the otter.

Even some species of the small insect-eating bats leave feeding signs in the form of moth wings and beetle elytra below hunting perches. Note the insect remains as well as the characteristic droppings.

Holes in the ground

Many different animals dig holes in the ground to gain access to food. In some cases the identification of the excavator is relatively easy but in many others one has to look for additional clues such as tracks and the type of food taken.

The title of master digger must go to the aardvark, a species that is widespread and leaves its holes for all to see. This animal is normally nocturnal but during severe drought it will forage by day. Deep claw marks are characteristic of its ground diggings and fragments of "termite clay" are usually scattered near the holes.

194

When digging the aardvark frequently uses its tail as a support and this leaves a distinct wedge-shaped track in the soil.

The most characteristic feeding sign left by the aardvark is the holes excavated into the sides of termite mounds.

Dung beetle brood-balls dug out by a honey badger and bitten open to gain access to the grubs.

Porcupines obtain most of their food by digging. In this case a large bulb was exposed and eaten. Note the clear track in the excavated soil and the remains of the bulb. Claw marks are often visible in such holes but these are never as large as those made by the aardvark.

Shallow excavations dug by a porcupine to gain access to small bulbs. It can be clearly seen that the bulbs have been bitten off.

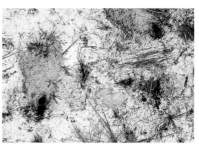

Holes dug by the bat-eared fox are rarely more than 70 mm across because it digs with the front paws held very close together. Several mongoose species are also frequent diggers but their feeding holes are always smaller than those of the bat-eared fox. You will need to search for tracks and other signs to identify the origins of this type of hole.

The bushpig is a frequent digger, but usually close to the surface. The tough snout is used to excavate soil and snout imprints may be found in the loosened earth. Much of the digging is to gain access to roots, bulbs and stems but insects are also commonly taken. These excavations can be extensive and cover many square metres. The baboon will also turn earth sods over large areas.

Grass dug out by a bushpig to gain access to the roots; note the track in the foreground.

Francolins and guineafowl dig a great deal when feeding, either by scuffing with the feet or using the beak, which usually leaves neat V-shaped holes only a little larger than it.

Feeding site used by Cape francolin; it had also been used as a dust-bath.

Corm skins discarded by Cape francolin.

Tree damage

Many species obtain all or part of their food from trees. The following photographs illustrate only the most obvious signs.

Elephants frequently feed on tree bark. In most cases the tusks are used to loosen bark which is then pulled off in strips with the trunk. No other species strips bark as extensively as the elephant.

The porcupine commonly ring-barks trees, with some tree species being most frequently attacked. Bark is rarely eaten above 60 cm. Fresh feeding signs are characterised by marks left by the large incisors.

Some species that do not normally eat bark, turn to it as a source of food during periods of food shortage. This bark was removed by a greater kudu. Antelope use the incisors on the lower jaw to strip bark.

Bark removed from a branch by a hyrax. These animals leave sharp grooves in the wood under the stripped-off bark.

Trees are frequently pushed over by elephants, usually to gain access to twigs, fruit and leaves but they also feed on the exposed roots. In areas of high elephant density many trees may be toppled.

When elephants feed on twigs these are usually torn off the tree, leaving ragged ends.

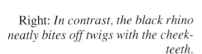

Right: *In contrast, the black rhino neatly bites off twigs with the cheek-teeth.*

Branches of an apple-leaf tree that had been broken up by an elephant. These pieces were then chewed to remove the bark, and the branches discarded.

An elephant used its forehead to shake loose the fruits of this palm.

Elephants frequently chew the tips of palm leaves but wads of the tough fibres are often not swallowed and these can be found scattered around in areas where palms grow.

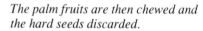

The palm fruits are then chewed and the hard seeds discarded.

Woodpeckers excavate nest-holes but also numerous smaller feeding holes in bark and wood when searching for insects. These shallow holes were made by a cardinal woodpecker.

Several small rodents strip the bark from tree saplings and kill many in this way. This specimen was ring-barked by a vlei rat.

Fruit and seeds

Fruit and seeds form an important part of the diet of many animals. Small fruit and seeds may be consumed whole but larger specimens may be only partly eaten. The method of feeding and the presence of tooth marks can provide important clues to the identity of the animal involved. Some animals are highly specialised feeders and eat, for example, only seeds, whereas others take only ripe fruits. You should always bear in mind that some species classified as carnivores also eat fruit from time to time.

An unripe tsamma melon bitten open and discarded by a brown hyaena. This animal eats the ripe fruit of several plants that occur within its range. The presence of tracks and the holes made in the fruit by the large canines provided the identification. You are most likely to see this kind of sign in the Kalahari.

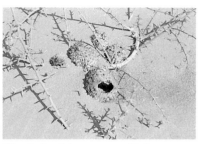

The fruit of the narra, which grows in the Namib Desert, provides a source of food for many species. In this case the fruit had been opened by a gerbil, as evidenced by tracks and the marks left by the incisors.

The monkey orange trees have a wide African distribution and their fruit is eaten by many species other than just monkeys. These fruits had been opened by vervet monkeys; only the pith around the large seeds is normally eaten.

This monkey orange had been opened by a monkey and further eaten by a giant rat. Note the marks left by the incisors.

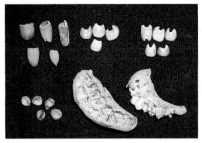

A small selection of seeds that had been partly eaten by small rodents. Clockwise from top left: multimammate mouse, multimammate mouse, Cape spiny mouse, tree mouse, striped mouse.

A number of bird species eat commercially grown fruit and considerable losses may result. These apricots were partly eaten by mousebirds. In nearly all cases marks left by the sharp beaks are diagnostic. Soft fruits are also frequently eaten by fruit bats; the fruit may be carried away from the tree or entirely consumed on it.

Grapes eaten by weavers; note that the fruit skins are still in place but the pith removed. Larger birds, such as the redwinged starling, may swallow grapes whole.

A maize cob that had been exposed and eaten by weavers. Individual seeds may be removed, or just hollowed out and left on the cob.

Although porcupines obtain most of their food by digging, they will also feed on surface plant material, such as this pumpkin. The marks left by the large incisors are clearly visible.

Other plant parts

Two types of rodent feed on the stems of reeds and sedges, the large greater canerat and the smaller vlei rats. They frequently occur in the same areas but can be differentiated on the size of cut reed sections and piles, as well as the presence of droppings. This photograph shows a cut stem pile as well as a sprinkling of the distinctive grooved droppings of the greater canerat.

Sedge stems cut into neat sections and the droppings of a vlei rat. Various species occur widely in Africa. These animals sometimes occur in large numbers and feeding piles may be found close to each other.

Baboons are often messy and destructive feeders. They eat a wide range of plants and other food. This stand of castor-oil bushes had been stripped and only the pith eaten. Look around such feeding signs for the distinctive tracks and droppings of this primate.

These aloe leaves had been pulled off the plant by a baboon but only a small portion of the fleshy bases eaten. Note the droppings of the red rock rabbit at centre.

A leopard tortoise had bitten off the tops of these succulent leaves. In this case droppings were present to confirm the identity but the lack of tooth marks ruled out most other herbivores.

The young growth tips of this euphorbia had been neatly nipped off and eaten by a klipspringer. Tracks were located nearby, as well as a latrine area.

The height of browse lines on trees and bushes can be an aid to identifying the browsers in an area.

The gerenuk, an antelope that can exploit a browsing level higher than many other species can reach, is restricted to the drier areas of east Africa

Insect feeding signs on plant material

The range of insect feeding signs is vast and we have selected only a few photographs to illustrate those signs that are most frequently encountered.

These leaves had been eaten by a large caterpillar but the locusts and grasshoppers also usually feed from the edge of a leaf towards its centre. Roughly circular pieces of leaf are cut and removed by cutter bees but the cut edges are usually quite neat. While feeding, caterpillars produce large numbers of small, oval droppings and substantial quantities may accumulate below large food plants.

Caterpillars feeding on the outer cells of a large, fleshy leaf. The inner layers may or may not be eaten.

The feeding galleries of leaf-miners, the caterpillars of small moths. They feed on the leaf cells of a wide range of plants. (Photo: Alan Weaving)

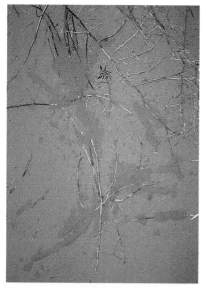

Two examples of the feeding tunnels of termites. The termites move under the clay layer where they break up the underlying vegetation. These tunnels are most abundant during the rains. (Right: Alan Weaving)

Harvester termites gather small pieces of cut grass, twigs and other plant material in roughly circular heaps near the entrances to their colonies.

Piles of fragmented wood outside holes excavated by large woodborer beetles.

Feeding tunnels excavated by the larvae of woodborer beetles, of which there are many species. Most feed between the bark and the wood.

Shallow water

Birds leave the most identifiable feeding signs in shallow water, although some fish leave marks on sandy and mud substrates and on algae-covered rocks. However, most observers will not encounter this type of sign.

Lesser flamingoes leave meandering trails in shallows, with the tracks usually straddling the trail. The trail is made by the upper surface of the bill.

Lesser flamingo feeding trail.

An attractive pattern created by feeding flamingoes. The water had dried several weeks earlier but the signs were still clearly visible. Greater flamingoes often feed by puddling the mud with their feet and this raises series of low mounds.

The feeding trail of an avocet; note the sabre-shaped sweeps in the sand on either side of the tracks.

6 NESTS AND SHELTERS

Many species of mammal, bird, reptile, amphibian and invertebrate construct or make use of some form of shelter. These shelters may be permanent, such as those made by termites, or temporary, as is the case with nearly all bird nests. The location of the shelter, materials used if any, size and structure can all give clues to the identity of the builder or occupier. Most shelters are well hidden or difficult to reach.

Some shelters may survive long after they had been vacated and signs of the occupiers in the way of tracks or dung will then no longer be present. The shelters of many small mammals are underground and only their entrances or excavated soil is visible on the surface. Under the surface there may be a short, simple tunnel ending in a nest chamber, or the tunnel system could be complex with many branches and several chambers, depending on the species. In most cases, however, we have to rely on those signs we see on the surface.

Each species, or group of closely related species, has its own method of removing the excavated soil. These methods can provide important clues to the identity of the inmates.

In this chapter we cover representative examples of bird nests and other animal shelters.

BIRD NESTS

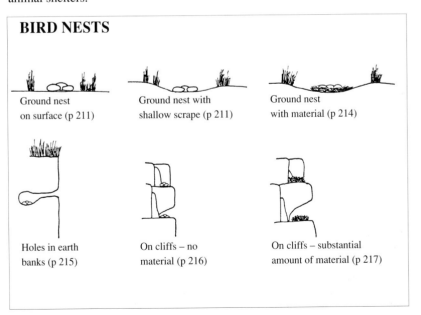

Ground nest
on surface (p 211)

Ground nest with
shallow scrape (p 211)

Ground nest
with material (p 214)

Holes in earth
banks (p 215)

On cliffs – no
material (p 216)

On cliffs – substantial
amount of material (p 217)

Nests in natural tree-holes (p 219)

Self-excavated tree-holes (p 220)

Self-excavated holes in nests of tree ants (p 221)

Nests floating on water (p 222)

Large dome-shaped nests in trees (p 222)

Small woven balls (p 224)

Long entrance spout (p 224)

Short entrance spout (p 226)

Very short or no entrance spout (p 226)

Finely woven with top, side entrance (p 227)

Coarse but tidy with top, side entrance (p 228)

Untidy with top, side entrance (p 229)

Felted with short side-tube (p 230)

Mud-pellet nests (p 231)

Cup-shaped, open (p 231)

Bowl-shaped, top entrance (p 232)

Bowl-shaped with entrance tunnel (p 232)

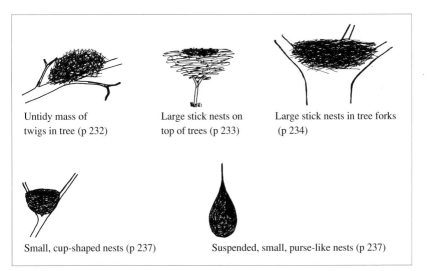

Untidy mass of twigs in tree (p 232)

Large stick nests on top of trees (p 233)

Large stick nests in tree forks (p 234)

Small, cup-shaped nests (p 237)

Suspended, small, purse-like nests (p 237)

It is not possible to describe the nests of all of the bird species that occur within the area covered by this book. We have selected representative nests that are typical of a particular group or family, or are distinctive, or frequently or easily seen. Documentation of the nests of all species is beyond the scope of this book: Zaïre is known to be home to at least 1 086 bird species, Kenya 1 067 and South Africa 774.

To identify a bird nest first check the key above, then look at the relevant section with its photographs and accompanying notes.

Ground nests – little or no material

This group of ground nests includes those of the ostrich, bustards, dikkops, coursers, pratincoles, plovers, terns, sandgrouse, nightjars and several owls. In general, once the eggs have hatched and the chicks left the nest there is little or no sign left to identify the species involved. Exceptions are the ostrich, which leaves large egg fragments that may remain for some time, and the ground-nesting owls which leave accumulations of regurgitated pellets and remains of prey items brought to the chicks.

Depending on the species the eggs may be laid directly on the ground (for example nightjars) or in a shallow scrape. In most cases no material is added to the scrape but some of the coursers may ring the nest with antelope or sheep droppings, or small stones. Despite the nests being mostly in fairly open areas they are difficult to locate: the eggs are well camouflaged, in most species the chicks leave the nest soon after hatching and the cryptic plumage of the adults blends well with their surroundings.

Species in this group occur widely in Africa. The terns are mainly restricted to the coastline.

The ostrich, the world's largest bird, lays large cream-coloured eggs in a shallow scrape in sandy soil. The eggs are 15 cm long and 13 cm in diameter. More than one hen may lay in the same nest, which may therefore contain more than 20 eggs. Ostriches are solitary nesters. They occur in many southern and east African game reserves.

The threebanded plover creates a shallow scrape and lines the nest with small flat stones and occasionally soil pieces and plant debris. The nest is usually on gravel or mud flats near water and contains one or two eggs. The threebanded plover occurs widely in southern and east Africa.

The whitefronted plover uses little or no lining in a shallow scrape. It occurs widely in sub-Saharan Africa.

A shallow scrape (about 10 cm in diameter) with sparse lining is typical of the Namaqua and other sandgrouse. Usually three eggs are laid.

With a few exceptions the francolins nest in shallow scrapes with sparse lining. The nest of the crested francolin is usually well hidden at the base of a grass clump.

The Cape francolin usually hides its nest under a bush or in dense vegetation but this nest was completely exposed at the base of a tree. The eggs hatched successfully.

Well-developed grass owl chicks at the nest. No material is used and the eggs are laid on flattened grass. Such sites can be recognised by the presence of pellets and prey remains and are located in dense grass cover. Like other owls the grass owl is solitary. It is widespread in suitable habitat in southern to east Africa. (Photo: John Carlyon)

213

Ground nests – fair amount of material

Many species using nests that belong to this group are associated with coastal or freshwater habitats. They include cormorants (which at inland waters usually nest in trees), ducks and geese, the white pelican and the gulls. Larks, pipits, longclaws and buntings are also primarily ground nesters, building mostly small but substantial nests that are difficult to locate.

The Cape cormorant constructs a shallow bowl of sticks, seaweed, feathers, plastic, string and other debris. These highly colonial cormorants are restricted to southern African coastal waters.

Usually a solitary nester, the black-winged stilt lines a scrape close to shallow inland waters. It occurs widely in Africa.

The kelp gull lines a shallow scrape with grass, seaweed, feathers and other material and lays two to three eggs. This gull, like other gulls, is colonial. It occurs in southern Africa.

Most ducks and geese are ground nesters and construct fairly large, down-lined nests. It is possible to identify most to species level by comparing down colour and patterning but this is beyond the scope of this book. This is the nest of the southern pochard (18 cm diameter), a widespread species.

214

A typical lark nest. Many lark species occur in the savanna and desert regions of Africa.

The Egyptian goose nests in a wide variety of locations in Africa, including on buildings, on cliffs, on old bird nests and on the ground. The nest usually has a dense lining of grey down. Goslings jump from considerable heights from the nest to the ground.

Self-excavated holes in vertical earth banks

Many kingfisher and bee-eater species excavate nest tunnels in vertical earth or sand banks, such as are found along river courses and erosion channels. Colonial breeders include some bee-eaters, martins and the pied starling, whereas kingfishers, the ground woodpecker and saw-wing swallows are solitary nesters. Some species excavate nesting burrows rapidly; others such as the martins and saw-wing swallows take much longer. An accumulation of droppings directly below each hole is a sign of active or recent occupation. Under holes occupied by kingfishers, and to a lesser extent bee-eaters, there are often small accumulations of regurgitated pellets if the nests are not directly above water.

215

Carmine bee-eaters form very large nesting colonies that are used each breeding season. Several such sites are located in major game parks in southern, central and east Africa.

The pied kingfisher is one of several species that excavate their own nest burrows. Accumulations of fish bones and scales are often found nearby.

Pied starling nest burrows. This species is found only in southern Africa.

On cliffs – little or no material

The nests in this group can be on coastal or montane cliffs, as well as on inselbergs. In many cases the nests are not clearly visible but can be located by the white streaks and accumulations directly below them. In the case of raptors and owls regurgitated pellets and prey remains are useful indicators. Several small raptors, including the peregrine and lanner falcons and the rock kestrel, owls such as the barn, spotted eagle and Cape (also Mackinder's) eagle owls, as well as the rock pigeon occupy nest sites on open ledges and small overhangs and in shallow caves.

216

Well-developed Cape eagle owl chicks. No nesting material is used but note the regurgitated pellets and prey remains. Cliff-nesting owls use the same sites for many years and there are often large accumulations of pellets and small bones from disintegrated pellets below such locations. (Photo: John Carlyon)

A rock pigeon nest with typical flimsy platform of fine twigs and pine needles. This species is widespread in sub-Saharan Africa.

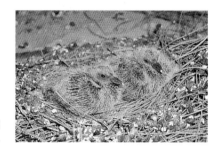

Well-developed rock pigeon squabs with nest circled by droppings.

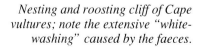

On cliffs – substantial nests

Some cliff-nesting species are colonial, such as the Cape and Rüppell's vultures (griffons), marabou stork and bald ibis, and this results in extensive "whitewashing" of nesting cliffs. Cliff-nesting vultures and the marabou have wide distributions but the bald ibis is restricted to southern Africa.

Solitary nesters include the black stork, black eagle, booted eagle, augur and jackal buzzards and whitenecked raven. All have wide distributions and most species return each year to the same breeding sites.

Nesting and roosting cliff of Cape vultures; note the extensive "whitewashing" caused by the faeces.

The bald ibis is a colonial nester. Each pair builds a fairly substantial structure (about 50 cm diameter) and nests often touch each other.

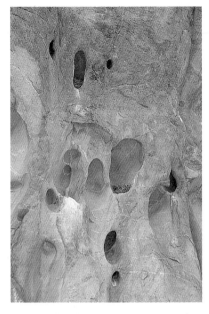

Eroded holes on cliff faces are used as nesting sites by many raptor species.

Black eagle nests are often massive (occasionally up to 4 m high) because the birds add to the structure every time they breed. The bowls of nests in use are lined with green plant material. As hyraxes form the bulk of the eagle's diet accumulations of this small mammal's skull and bones litter the area below the nest. (Photo: John Carlyon)

The black eagle constructs a large stick nest on a high cliff face; extensive "whitewashing" is visible directly below the nest.

Nests in natural tree-holes

A great number of bird species make use of natural tree-holes as nesting sites. This group includes the parrots, rollers, hoopoes, hornbills, trogons, several kingfishers, most tits, the glossy starlings, oxpeckers and the wood, scops and barred owls. Such holes may result from branches breaking, rot, fungal attack or lightning strikes. Very few species modify these holes, so little evidence is available to aid identification to group or species level. One exception is the hornbill. Many hornbill species select a suitable hole and the female seals herself in with mud provided by the male. A narrow slit is left through which the male feeds the female; when the chicks can readily accept food she breaks out and the young re-seal the entrance. They are fed by the adults until they fledge. The females of some species remain "imprisoned" until the young are fully fledged.

The hoopoe and the woodhoopoes, including the scimitarbilled woodhoopoe in the photograph, nest in natural tree-holes. They are widespread in sub-Saharan Africa.

Most African parrots nest in tree-holes, either those excavated by woodpeckers or barbets, or natural holes. Two of these holes were used by Rüppell' s parrots and had probably been excavated by a bearded woodpecker. The parrots have pulled off pieces of bark near the holes.

219

This woodland kingfisher is using an abandoned woodpecker hole. (Photo: John Carlyon)

A sealed grey hornbill nest-hole. Many hornbill species occur in sub-Saharan Africa.

Self-excavated holes in trees

The woodpeckers, barbets and tinker barbets excavate their own nest-holes, usually in dead trees or branches. Height from the ground varies considerably. The holes are usually neat and more or less circular. Tinker barbet holes are usually 2-3 cm in diameter and those of barbets and woodpeckers more than 5 cm. Nearly all these species are solitary nesters although several holes may be excavated in a suitable tree or branch.

Female goldentailed woodpecker at self-excavated nest-hole. (Photo: John Carlyon)

220

Nest-hole excavated by a cardinal woodpecker.

Blackcollared barbet at a self-excavated nest-hole. This barbet is widespread south of the Equator. (Photo: John Carlyon)

Pied barbet nest and feeding holes in the soft stem of a tree aloe.

Self-excavated holes in nests of tree ants

Although few bird species nest in arboreal ant nests, the distinct character of these nests warrants mention. None occur in southern Africa. A neat, circular hole in the side of a tree ant nest could indicate the presence of the chocolate-flanked kingfisher, buffspotted woodpecker or Macclounie's barbet.

221

Nests floating on water

Species that construct nests on water include the dabchick, grebes, redknobbed coot, jacanas and the whiskered tern. The nests are usually made up of aquatic plants and in the case of the coot these masses may be substantial, whereas the jacana nests are relatively sparse. Some are solitary nesters, others form loose colonies. Representatives are found throughout Africa.

The redknobbed coot constructs a substantial mound nest of water plants with a shallow cup in which the eggs are laid. This species occurs widely in Africa.

African jacana nest with a thin pad of vegetation. (Photo: John Carlyon)

A dabchick (little grebe) nest anchored to reeds. When leaving the nest the parent bird usually covers the eggs with vegetation. (Photo: John Carlyon)

Large dome-shaped nests in trees

Only two species build nests that fall into this category, the sociable weaver, which is restricted to the arid west of southern Africa and the hamerkop, which occurs widely in sub-Saharan Africa. The pygmy falcon in southern Africa nests in an empty chamber in a colonial sociable weaver nest. Such chambers can be identified by the coating of white droppings around the entrance.

A group of sociable weaver nests in a large acacia tree. Up to 50 separate nest chambers may be constructed from dry grass stalks and the whole roofed with coarse plant material. This is probably the most visible of all African bird nests.

In areas where large trees are few and far between sociable weavers construct their nests on telegraph poles: a common sight throughout their range.

The hamerkop builds a massive, domed, oven-shaped nest that may be 2 m in diameter. The nest is constructed from twigs, reeds and often human litter such as plastic, cloth and string. One nest in the grounds of a hospital is decorated with old drip tubes, plastic gloves and bandages. The nest in the photograph is typical. Nests are also frequently made on cliff ledges.

Hamerkop nests are frequently used by other birds for breeding, in this case a barn owl. Other species, such as the Egyptian goose and the giant eagle owl, often nest on top of the dome.

Small woven balls

This group includes many of the most frequently seen and most distinctive bird nests. They are constructed by the true weavers, sparrow-weavers, sparrows, prinias, cisticolas, apalises, sunbirds and penduline tits. Although many of the species are solitary nesters, several of the true weavers, the queleas and the sparrow-weavers are colonial. In some species, such as queleas, colonies may consist of hundreds of nests. Typical examples of the different groups are presented in the following photographs.

Long entrance spout

This group consists of weaver nests with an entrance spout exceeding 20 cm in length. They are usually solitary. Species include the forest, spectacled and redheaded weavers, all of which have extensive distributions.

Nest of a forest weaver.

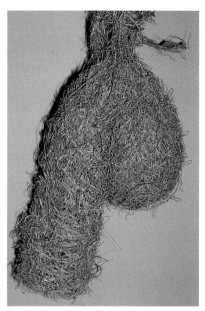

Nest of a spectacled weaver.

Although redheaded weavers are usually solitary nesters they occasionally form small colonies. (Photo: Penny Meakin)

Occasionally one nest is built below another.

Short entrance spout

The Cape, lesser masked, golden and chestnut weavers all have nests with a short entrance spout (3-10 cm). With the exception of the golden weaver all are colonial nesters.

A lesser masked weaver male putting finishing touches to the nest.

Very short or no entrance spout

The widely distributed and colonial spottedbacked, masked, yellow and brownthroated weavers build nests with a very short or no entrance spout.

Spottedbacked weaver colony.

226

Masked weaver colony.

Yellow weaver nest clearly showing the absence of an entrance spout.

Nests of the blackcapped social weaver, a particularly common species in northern Kenya, are found in tight clusters. The nests are tidier than those of the whitebrowed sparrow-weaver with which it frequently shares trees when nesting.

Finely woven with top, side entrance

The thickbilled weaver constructs a finely woven nest of grass, reed strips or lengths of palm leaf, commonly in reedbeds. This usually colonial species is widespread in sub-Saharan Africa.

227

Nests in this group are built by the queleas, bishops, prinias, cisticolas, apalises and sunbirds (those of the latter four are more properly oval in shape). Representatives of all these families are widespread in Africa south of the Sahara. With the exception of those of the queleas and colonial bishops, the nests are usually well hidden and not easily found.

Part of a redbilled quelea colony; such colonies are often huge with many neighbouring trees each holding several hundred nests.

The yellowrumped widow (Cape bishop) is a solitary nester although a male may build several nests a few metres apart. The entrance usually has a small porch. The nest of the red bishop is similar but this bishop breeds in colonies.

Nest of a Neergaard's sunbird. Two groups of sunbird nests can be distinguished, those with and those without a porched side-top entrance. Lichens, fine vegetation and cobwebs are used in nest construction.

Malachite sunbird nest.

The Karoo (spotted) prinia constructs a neat nest close to the ground; the structure is of grass and lined with plant down.

Nest of a rufouseared warbler. In most cases involving the prinias, cisticolas and warblers it is difficult to identify the builder on nest structure alone.

Untidy with top, side entrance

Several species build nests that belong to this category but most are well hidden and difficult to locate, such as those of the waxbills and firefinches. A few species, such as the Cape, house and great sparrows construct untidy balls of plant material and other debris usually located in trees or bushes.

The untidy ball constructed by a Cape sparrow. It usually nests in small colonies.

Whitebrowed sparrow-weavers occur from South Africa into east Africa. They are colonial breeders that construct an untidy ball of grass stems with a side tunnel.

A whitebrowed sparrow-weaver nest.

Felted with short side-tube

The penduline tits (several species in Africa) construct a unique nest of felted animal and plant fibres that cannot be mistaken for the nest of any other species. A flap above the entrance can beopened and closed. The nest is approximately15 cm high.

Nest of a Cape penduline tit; note the closed entrance and the ledge below it on which the parent bird would stand.

Mud-pellet nests

Nearly all of the birds that build nests with mud pellets belong to the swallow and martin group. The nests can be divided into three groups: open cup-shaped nests, closed bowls with a top, side entrance hole and closed bowls with a long side tunnel. Many species often nest in association with human habitation. Some thrushes line the nest cup with mud, the palm thrushes construct a cup-shaped shell of mud that is lined with woven palm-leaf fibres and the redwinged starling builds a circle of mud on which the nest is constructed. Swallows, martins and thrushes occur throughout Africa, but the redwinged starling is restricted to southern Africa.

The rock martin constructs an open cup attached to a wall or sheltered rock face. Other species that nest in this way are the pearlbreasted, whitethroated and wiretailed swallows. The last species mixes the mud with grass. These species are solitary nesters.

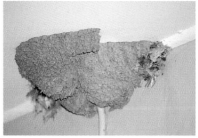

*South African cliff swallows con-
struct closed bowls of mud with a
top, side entrance. Many nests may
be built close together.*

*Nests of greater striped swallows
are characterised by a long entrance
tunnel, as are those built by lesser
striped, mosque (often on baobab
trees) and redbreasted swallows.
The nests in the photograph have
been taken over by house sparrows
as indicated by the feathers sticking
out of the entrances.*

*A greater striped swallow nest
attached to the inner surface of a
thatched roof.*

*The nest of a redwinged starling
showing its mud base. (Photo: John
Carlyon)*

Untidy mass of twigs in tree

Two birds construct nests belonging to this group,
the wattled starling and the redbilled buffalo weaver.
Both species are widespread from southern to east
Africa.

232

The redbilled buffalo weaver builds a large, untidy communal stick structure with two or more vertical entrances. Several such structures may be located in a single tree. Nests may also be seen on windmills and telephone poles.

Nests of buffalo weavers provide suitable structures for nesting by other species, such as this giant eagle owl.

Large stick nests on top of trees

Several birds construct large stick platforms from 1-3 m in diameter in trees. The white, marabou and saddlebilled storks, the lappetfaced vulture, secretarybird and tawny eagle all build tree-top nests. These nests are often surprisingly difficult to spot from the ground despite their large size. Other species that frequently construct their nests (50 cm to 1 m) in tree crowns are the yellowbilled stork and several raptors including the hooded vulture and African hawk eagle. There are usually accumulations of regurgitated pellets below active, or recently vacated, nests of raptors.

233

The weight of this lappetfaced vulture nest caused it to collapse below the tree crown. New material is added each breeding season. This species occurs widely in Africa and is a solitary nester.

The white stork constructs a large stick nest usually located on top of a tree. Small numbers breed along southern Cape Province coast and in north-western Africa.

Large to medium stick nests in tree forks or on horizontal branches

Many species of bird build their nests in trees, most notably in forks or on horizontal branches. They include many raptors, herons and crows. The following are just a few examples of such nests.

The whitebacked vulture is a common savanna species that builds a relatively small nest for its size. It also builds on top of smaller trees. (Photo: John Carlyon)

The crowned eagle constructs its massive stick nest in a large forest tree. As is common with many raptors, green plant material is regularly brought to "decorate" the bowl and nest rim. Large accumulations of prey bones are found below active nests – these come from monkeys, small antelope and hyraxes. This eagle is found in forest throughout tropical Africa and as far south as the eastern Cape Province. (Photo: John Carlyon)

Many of the smaller raptors, including the sparrowhawks and goshawks, build stick nests in tree forks. This nest of a little sparrowhawk is typical. (Photo: John Carlyon)

Whitebreasted cormorants nest communally and usually in trees on inland waters. Typical of many large colonial-nesting birds is the large quantity of white faeces which may eventually kill the tree.

A tree that has been killed by the faeces of nesting whitebreasted cormorants and other waterbirds. They also nest in drowned trees.

Cattle egrets are colonial nesters and occur widely in sub-Saharan Africa. Colonies are usually associated with lakes, rivers or marshes.

The greenbacked heron constructs a flimsy, almost dove-like structure of twigs. It nests solitarily or in small colonies. Nests are normally located towards the end of a horizontal branch. (Photo: John Carlyon)

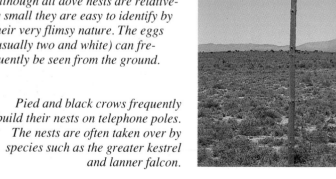

Although all dove nests are relatively small they are easy to identify by their very flimsy nature. The eggs (usually two and white) can frequently be seen from the ground.

Pied and black crows frequently build their nests on telephone poles. The nests are often taken over by species such as the greater kestrel and lanner falcon.

Small, cup-shaped nests in trees or bushes

Many of the smaller birds construct cup-shaped nests. They include mousebirds, drongos, babblers, bulbuls, thrushes, robins, flycatchers, shrikes, white-eyes, canaries and buntings. Although certain characteristics can be used to distinguish the nests of some species the average observer would have great difficulty in differentiating one from another.

A Heuglin's robin at its parasitised nest, feeding a redchested cuckoo chick. (Photo: John Carlyon)

Paradise flycatchers, like other fly-catchers, use spiderweb to bind their nests. Bits of lichen are frequently incorporated. (Photo: John Carlyon)

Suspended, small, purse-like nests

The tiny crombecs build a unique, suspended purse-like nest. They are widespread in Africa.

Nest of a longbilled crombec; note the suspended bag decorated with pieces of lichen.

237

MAMMAL SHELTERS

Many species of mammal do not construct or use a permanent shelter, but merely lie up where they happen to be at the time. Signs of their resting may include flattened grass or slight impressions in dust and sand. To identify the animal that rested at such a site is generally difficult and one must search for additional clues such as tracks and droppings. Like birds, many mammals make use of shelters only when they have dependent young. Mammal shelters can be broadly divided into those in trees, on the ground and in burrows below the ground.

In trees and bushes

By far the greatest number of mammals that rest or shelter in trees make no attempt to construct nests and apart from accumulations of droppings there is little indication of the species involved.

Some species of the large fruit-eating bats roost, often in large numbers, in the same trees every day. Their soft droppings and urine are very acidic and stain the ground and the vegetation below the roost. Such roosts are located in a number of towns and cities in tropical Africa. Several species of the smaller insect-eating bats make use of holes in trees (baobabs are favoured). Hole roosts can be identified by the accumulations of small droppings and grease marks at the entrances.

Most primate species sleep in trees, including the savanna baboon and the typical monkeys. Only the gorilla, chimpanzee, bonobo and some of the bushbabies construct nests. The common chimpanzee constructs a nest that can be distinguished from a large bird nest because branches are bent or partly broken, and intertwined to form a platform. This is usually lined with twigs and leaves to form a ring around the chimpanzee. A new nest is constructed each night, usually 5-40 m above the ground. However, in parts of eastern Zaïre chimpanzees have been recorded constructing nests on the ground. Apart from northern and eastern Zaïre, chimpanzees may be encountered in western Uganda and Tanzania, as well as in scattered areas of west Africa.

The untidy leaf and twig nest of a thick-tailed bushbaby. These nests are usually difficult to locate as they are often in dense vegetation tangles. The smaller bushbaby species may also construct their own nests but lesser bushbaby nests are usually not covered. A number of the tree squirrels construct similar leaf nests.

Although both lowland and mountain gorilla females and young may construct crude, roughly circular platforms of branches in trees, nests of shrubs and herbs may also be made on the ground. The heavy adult males nearly always sleep on the ground, in this posture. Note the pile of droppings at the edge of the nest. Gorillas are restricted to the tropical forest zone and are found only as far east as the border between Zaïre and Uganda. (Photo: Harry van Rompaey)

Tree hyraxes use natural tree holes for nests, as do tree squirrels (some species construct leaf nests, called dreys, which resemble those of the bushbabies). Tree holes are also occasionally used by the genets and by several mouse and rat species.

On the ground

Many mammals rest on the ground but as previously mentioned they leave little sign of it. These include all the antelope (although some of the solitary species may use favoured resting sites), the hares and many of the larger carnivores, such as lion and cheetah. Young remain under cover until they are able to follow the mother; at such sites droppings and tracks may indicate the presence of a hidden shelter. The sow of the widespread bushpig either constructs a mound of dry grass (about 3 m in diameter and over 1 m high) in dense cover, in which she gives birth, or makes use of existing cover such as fallen branches and rock piles. A number of the smaller rodents and the shrews construct ball-shaped or cupped nests in dense vegetation cover, usually in grass or reeds. However, unless you go in search of these nests you are unlikely to see them. A few other rodents, such as the Karoo bush rat and Namaqua rock mouse, construct large surface structures of vegetation which disguise the entrances to their shelters.

239

A bushbuck fawn lair. The young of several antelope species remain hidden for a few weeks to months and the vegetation may become very trampled. One should look for associated tracks and other signs.

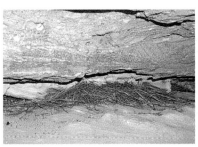

The Namaqua rock mouse (widespread in southern Africa) usually lives in deep rock crevices and scree and the entrances can be identified by the accumulations of plant debris.

Karoo bush rats construct large (up to 1,5 m by 1,2 m) surface nests with sticks that vary greatly in length (up to 50 cm). There are nesting chambers in the mound. Subsurface burrows are hidden by the mound and surface trails radiate to feeding sites. This species is restricted to southern Africa south of the Orange River.

A brown hyaena den in dense vegetation; note the accumulation of white droppings to the side of the shelter entrance. Brown hyaenas also make use of burrows in some areas.

Underground

A wide range of mammals dig burrows in the ground, or use holes constructed by other species. In order to excavate or modify these burrows the animals have to remove the soil, and the way in which this is done can assist you to identify the species involved. Where the entrance hole is located, its

240

diameter and any associated tracks and droppings can also provide important clues. The entrances to old, unused systems soon start to collapse and spiders spin webs across the holes, with dry plant debris usually present.

The burrows of the small colonial rodents are usually easy to locate but those of the many solitary burrowing species are difficult to find and identify. In order to narrow down the identities of burrow excavators you have to note the locality and habitat in which a hole is found. For example, if you find burrow entrances with a diameter of some 19 cm in forest or dense woodland, they could be those excavated by the giant rat. If in the arid southwest you locate neat, round, almost vertical holes measuring some 2 cm they could be those of the large-eared mouse. However, one needs considerable field experience to identify burrow excavators positively.

The following photographs provide a general guide to the types of burrows and surface activity that you are most likely to encounter.

The subsurface ridges created by golden moles usually radiate from deep nest chambers and are created during foraging. Golden moles , which occur widely in sub-Saharan Africa, are most abundant in sand and loamy soils, and are most active after rain.

The rodent molerats excavate extensive tunnel systems, and surplus soil is pushed to the surface in mounds. The root rats of east Africa do the same. They show a preference for lighter soils but in some areas clay soils are occupied, from sea-level to high mountains. These mounds were pushed up by the Damara molerat and are up to 30 cm high and 50-70 cm in diameter; the mounds are often smaller. Most mounds are pushed up during and after rain.

Root rats push up fairly large mounds of loose sub-soil, frequently in montane forest clearings (especially at such locales as the Mount Kenya sub-alpine zone). These species are not found in southern Africa.

The largest mounds (up to 50 cm high) are pushed up by the Cape dune molerat, but this species is restricted to coastal southern and western South Africa These mounds are easily seen alongside many roads in the area.

When the soil is damp the earth on fresh mounds retains the cylindrical form of the tunnel of the common molerat.

A Cape molerat mound pushed up in very dry soil.

Naked molerats (sand-puppies) are restricted to the drier areas of Kenya, Somalia and Ethiopia, and they push up a characteristic "volcanic cone" mound.

The dwarf mongoose shelters in old termite mounds and their ventilation shafts, as does the banded mongoose. Accumulations of their droppings are often found close by. Both species have wide distributions but are absent from the arid south-west, favouring woodland savanna.

The suricate is an active digger, both of shelters and when foraging. It is restricted to the arid south-west.

A small yellow mongoose warren that has long been in use, as indicated by its raised level. This species is restricted to southern Africa.

A colonial species, the suricate shows a preference for excavating its warren systems in hard or stony substrate. The warren sites may eventually become raised above the level of the surrounding ground. Entrance holes are 8-15 cm in diameter. Small accumulations of droppings are usually present. Suricates may share warrens with the yellow mongoose and ground squirrels, where they occur together.

A hole (known as a holt) excavated by a Cape clawless otter in sandy alluvial soil; where otters excavate in a riverbank they may dig a second hole which emerges in the vegetation above the bank. Holt entrances are generally oval and are 36 cm across and 25 cm high. Those excavated by the spotted-necked otter are smaller (20 cm by 13 cm). Both species also shelter in dense vegetation cover, such as reedbeds. Note the accumulations of scats in the foreground and top left. (Photo: Dave Rowe-Rowe)

The aardwolf may excavate its own burrow, or modify those dug by other species such as the springhare, porcupine and aardvark. The entrance is usually about 40 cm wide and 30 cm high if the burrow is self-excavated or a modified springhare hole. Accumulations of large, dark droppings are often located near the burrow.

The aardvark, widely distributed in sub-Saharan Africa, excavates a very large burrow, with the entrance up to 1 m in diameter. The massive claws on the front feet leave deep grooves in the wall of the burrow. The burrows may be relatively short and temporary, or much deeper, permanent and complex systems that usually have several entrances. Occupied burrows usually have swarms of tiny flies in the entrances.

Warthogs, a species of open wood-land and savanna, modify holes dug by the aardvark and porcupines but will also make use of culverts. They occasionally dig their own simple burrow in soft soil. Dry grass is sometimes carried to the chamber if it contains newborn piglets and this may litter the entrance.

Porcupines frequently excavate their own burrows but also use aardvark burrows and natural cover such as rock piles, caves and dense vegeta-tion. Regularly used shelters are characterised by accumulations of gnawed bones and distinctive shed quills. This is a self-excavated bur-row.

A newly opened springhare burrow with extensive fan of excavated earth, which may have a radius of 1,5 m. Entrance holes are usually 18-25 cm in diameter. There may be several entrance holes to the extensive system, with one vertical exit hole lacking the soil fan. Only a single springhare, or a female with young, occupies each system but loose colonies are formed. Colonies are located in well-drained, compact sandy soils. The holes with fans are often plugged from the inside during the day. Note the tracks left by the hind feet of an animal that has entered the burrow.

The southern ground squirrel lives in colonies in open, arid terrain. Some colonies may contain about 32 animals but many are smaller. It digs extensive burrow systems in hard substrate. Continuous digging eventually raises the warren above the surrounding ground. Entrances are 10-15 cm in diameter but height is usually less than width. The holes are characterised by a crater-shaped mound of freshly excavated soil.

Colonies of Brant's whistling rat can be seen in the arid south-west of southern Africa. They are usually located in dry, coarse, sandy soils, mainly in plains between sand dunes and in dry riverbeds. Each individual system may have more than 20 entrances, each with a diameter of about 8 cm. Some of the largest colonies can be observed in the Kalahari Gemsbok National Park (South Africa). As in this photograph, entrances become littered with inedible plant remains discarded by these rodents, as well as accumulations of droppings.

The small hairy-footed gerbils of southern Africa dig their burrows at the base of perennial vegetation. Systems usually only have one entrance which has a ramp of loose soil on the surface. In the loose sands of the Namib Desert these gerbils dig where gemsbok urine has consolidated the surface. The diameter of the entrance hole is 3-4 cm.

Burrow of a brush-tailed hairy-footed gerbil; note all the tracks.

The Tatera *group of gerbils are widespread in Africa and usually live in small to very large colonies, depending on the species. This is a burrow of the bushveld gerbil in sandy soil. A burrow is usually 4-4,5 cm in diameter. Fresh ramps of soil at the entrance are usual; note the accumulations of seed husks.*

Entrances to the burrows of Cape gerbils are often at the base of vege-tation, but not always. These gerbils are commonly associated with culti-vated lands. Entrance holes are 5-7 cm in diameter and there is usu-ally freshly excavated soil.

INVERTEBRATE SHELTERS

Some of the most complex shelters are constructed by termites, ants, bees and wasps. Many species are highly social and their societies and shelters function in much the same way as human settlements. Although in most cases the intricate structures are hidden from our view it is often possible to identify the group of insects or other invertebrates responsible for them.

Virtually throughout Africa the most visible and regularly seen shelters are those constructed by termites (incorrectly called white ants by many people). They are to be found in most habitats and take many forms, from very little surface signs to mighty castles of clay.

The harvester termites (Hodotermes spp.) create loose mounds of earth pellets that are rarely higher than a few centimetres. Another characteristic of this group is the small piles of cut grass stems and leaves surrounding entrance holes. The darker patches in the photograph consist of freshly excavated soil.

The mounds of the snouted harvester termites (Trinovertermes spp.) are a common feature of the African landscape, particularly savanna. Most mounds are 50 cm high but some may reach 100 cm. Similar mounds (about 35 cm high) are constructed by the black mound termites but as their name implies their "castles of clay" are usually black. These termites eat humus and wood.

An abandoned and weathered termite mound, revealing the internal passages. Abandoned mounds weather slowly and may last many years.

A snouted harvester termite mound showing the dark, freshly added soil-saliva mixture. This soon dries and lightens in colour.

Snouted harvester termites adding to the mound; most building takes place in the rainy season.

Some of the fungus-growing termites (for example Macrotermes *spp.*) construct very large surface mounds that are a common feature of Africa. The mounds may be tall and pointed as in the photograph, or huge and rounded. Odontotermes *species are also fungus growers.*

Some termites, including the fungus growers (Odontotermes *spp.*), construct ventilation shafts to control the temperature in their underground "cities". These shafts are used as shelter by many vertebrate and invertebrate species, such as this skink.

A mound with several ventilation shafts, created by fungus-growing termites. This type is common in Kenya.

In the forests of tropical Africa the termite Cubitermes speciosus *constructs a unique mound that resembles a multicapped mushroom, with up to five caps. These act as umbrellas to deflect the copious rains that fall in these areas.*

249

Ants also have complex social systems but many species live in colonies well hidden from sight: deep underground, under rocks or logs or among dense vegetation. There are however a number of notable exceptions.

*Among the most visible of ant nests are those constructed by the cocktail ants (*Crematogaster *spp.). Depending on the species the spherical or oval plant fibre nests are located in trees, bushes, stands of reeds or long coarse grass. These ants are widespread in Africa and very aggressive when disturbed.*

The entrance holes and debris excavated by harvester ants, with inedible seed husks and other plant material. Note the distinct foraging trails radiating from the colony. The mound in the background was constructed by snouted harvester termites. Harvester ants bring out seeds to dry in the sun before returning them to underground storage chambers.

These large Camponotus *sp. ants are living in a hole at the base of a snouted termite mound.*

A number of ant species pile debris from their underground colonies around the entrance holes; this is the work of a Camponotus *ant colony photographed in the Kalahari.*

*Rings of excavated soil on the surface of a colony of the brown house ant (*Pheidole *sp.).*

The wasps are among the most accomplished insect architects; some build brood chambers from mud, others from chewed plant fibres. Many wasps are solitary, others live in small colonies.

The nests in the following photographs had been constructed by paper wasps (*Belonogaster* spp.). The larvae, each in an individual cell, are fed on chewed caterpillars or other insects by the females. Nests are commonly built on buildings, in trees and bushes or hanging from rocks. The wasps are very aggressive when disturbed and can deliver an excruciating sting.

Paper wasps.

The cells that are closed contain pupating young.

251

Paper wasps.

Many species of wasp construct nests of mud, others construct underground chambers with elaborate mud entrance tunnels. The following photographs illustrate just a few.

The multi-chambered nest of a Sceliphron *sp. wasp; these nests may reach lengths of as much as 20 cm. Each chamber is packed with paralysed spiders and one egg is laid in each chamber. These mud nests are commonly found in buildings, on rocks and in trees throughout Africa.*

*An entrance tube to the nest of a mason wasp (*Odynerus *sp.); note the wet ring of fresh mud being added to the mouth of the tube by the wasp. These wasps stock their nests with paralysed caterpillars.*

252

The completed entrance tube to a mason wasp nest. (Photo: Alan Weaving)

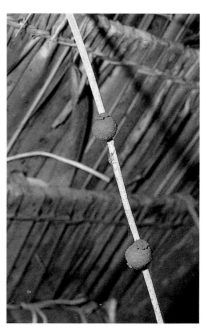

Two single-cell nests of a potter wasp (the mason and potter wasps belong to the family Eumenidae). Each mud pot is stocked with para lysed caterpillars and one egg is laid in each. The pots are usually 1-2 cm in diameter. (Photo: Alan Weaving)

Bees, particularly the honey bees, usually have well-hidden hives, either underground, in deep rock crevices, in holes in trees or in other cavities. There are a number of solitary species.

Entrance hole with soil pellet rings of one of the burrowing bees.

One of the most frequently encountered insect shelters in many drier parts of Africa is the conical pit constructed by the larva of the antlion (Family Myrmeleontidae). The pits are usually about 3 cm in diameter at the top and 2-3 cm deep. A single large-jawed larva remains buried under the pit, waiting for an unsuspecting insect to fall into it, where it is promptly seized and eaten. Pits are usually found in groups, with larva trails meandering over the area.

A group of pits excavated by antlion larvae.

The steep-sided pit excavated by an antlion larva.

The shelters constructed by two marine crabs (Crustaceae) warrant mention as they are abundant and obvious.

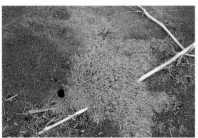

The ghost crabs (Ocypode spp.) are common on sandy beaches, particularly in the African tropics, and they construct burrows that are distinguished by the numerous tracks around the entrance. Burrows are located near the high-water mark and there may be many close together.

The red mangrove crab (Sesarma sp.) excavates a hooded burrow, which is one of the most frequent shelters found in mangrove swamps. Note the pellets of excavated mud and the slight overhang over the entrance. The entrances are up to 12 cm in diameter.

Another skilful builder is the larva of the bagworm moths (Psychidae), which are widespread in Africa. The larva may build a "mobile home" of cut twig segments, small stones, sand grains, pieces of leaves and small shells.

The "mobile home" of a bagworm moth larva.

Bagworm. (Photo: Alan Weaving)   *Bagworm. (Photo: Alan Weaving)*

Other invertebrates that construct well-known shelters are the spiders. In many cases these "shelters" are sophisticated hunting traps, in the form of the silken webs which the spiders spin to ensnare their insect prey. The following photographs show only a small number of the known forms but include the ones most commonly encountered.

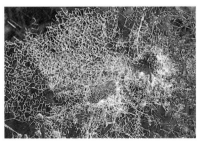

A web constructed and occupied by communal-living spiders (Family Eresidae). These large webs are a common sight.

Another communal-spider web. It should be noted that the caterpillars of some moths spin communal webs over their food plants.

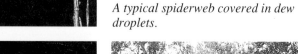

A web spun by a kite spider (Gasteracantha *sp.*) across a forest path.

A typical spiderweb covered in dew droplets.

The large, multilayered web of a tropical tent-spider (Cyrtophora *sp.*).

A large female orb spider showing the golden-coloured thread that typifies the webs of golden orb spiders.

The entrance to this baboon spider tunnel was 3,5 cm in diameter. The shelters of some species do not extend beyond the surface.

*The egg sac and nursery for the spiderlings of the rain spider (*Palystes castaneus*) are a common sight and are constructed of leaves and finely woven webbing.*

The retreat of a funnel-web spider. There are many species, each with its distinctive web form. This individual had taken over a hole excavated by a woodborer beetle.

A Palystes *sp. spider defending her egg sac. This nest was made of web silk and no plant material was included. The females of these spiders remain close to the nests and defend them vigorously. The egg sacs are usually quite large, many exceeding 8 cm in length.*

The retreats of one of the rock rain spiders (Olios spp.); these are of tough webbing and are usually located under rocks.

Praying mantis (Order Mantodea) females about to lay eggs secrete a gum-like liquid that has a consistency like silk. On contact with the air it turns into foam and she molds it into shape (which varies according to species), laying the eggs in the centre, each in its own chamber. The foam hardens and is remarkably tough. The nests are usually attached to vegetation or rocks.

Two large praying mantis egg-cases (these were 7 cm and 8 cm long but many are much smaller).

Newly hatched mantises on the egg-case. Note the polystyrene-like structure of the egg-case.

A foam nest of over 10 cm is constructed by the grey tree frog (also known as the foam-nest tree frog). The female secretes a substance which she and attendant males beat into a foam. It has the appearance of whipped cream and produces a safe, moist nest for the eggs and the early tadpole stages. These nests, attached to branches or other vegetation above water, are produced during the rains. They are a common sight in the tropics and subtropics.

A fresh grey tree frog foam-nest. The tadpoles drop from the nest to the water below.

Many lizard species live in holes in the ground but most use those dug by other animals, such as rodents. The barking geckoes (*Ptenopus* spp.) live in loose, sometimes large, colonies, each excavating its own burrow. The entrances are oval, roughly 2 cm wide and 1 cm high. Burrows are most commonly in sandy flats, such as riverbeds, in the arid west of southern Africa.

Burrow of a barking gecko.

7 OTHER SIGNS

This chapter deals with those signs that do not fit into earlier chapters but are frequently encountered in the field.

Mud-wallowing

A number of mammals are fond of mud-wallowing, particularly on warm days, and follow this with a good rub and scratch on a tree, rock or termite mound. The wallows may remain for long periods, depending on the traffic at any particular water-hole or mud-bath. Certain wallows may be favoured and as they deepen with use develop into semi-permanent water-holes. The wet mud serves as a cooling agent and provides some temporary relief from swarms of biting flies.

Rhinos make frequent use of mud-wallows and because of their size leave substantial depressions in the mud. We have seen wallows in fine silt-mud that retained clear outlines of the rhinos long after the mud had dried.

The height of mud rubbed off on trees can give an indication of the species involved, but always bear in mind the variation in any particular species. A white rhino used this tree as a rubbing post. The shoulder height of those species that most frequently wallow and rub is roughly: elephant 2,5-3,4 m; white rhino 1,8 m; black rhino 1,6 m; buffalo 1,4 m and warthog 65 cm.

A wallowing session is usually followed by a good scratch, which leaves some mud on the rubbing post.

The dried-out wallow and adjacent rubbing post of a black rhino. The rubbing posts of mud-wallowers are nearly always close to the wallow. Mud often remains on the tree for many months, particularly on ones in regular use.

One should always be aware that a large wallower, such as this black rhino, may rub the head at a lower level and then move to another tree for a body scratch. As this could cause confusion, have a good look at the other trees in the vicinity.

261

This stone was in regular use as a "belly-rub" by several white rhinos; note the trampled vegetation around the stone. Some rubbing stones remain in use for many years and become smoothly polished.

An elephant rubbing tree; no other species rubs to this height. This tree is obviously in regular use as indicated by the trampled vegetation and the thickness of the mud layer on the bark. Although young elephant often wallow, adults usually splash the mud on to their bodies with the trunk.

A 2,2 m tall termite mound that has been partly smoothed by an elephant.

Some rubbing posts are regularly used.

A tree stump that has become highly polished by the rubbing of many elephants.

An old mud-rub left by buffalo.

Most members of the pig family wallow, like this sounder of giant forest hog. Although the bushpig and warthog are widely distributed, the giant forest hog is restricted to the tropical forest zone. (Photo: Roland van Bocxstaele)

The warthog can probably claim the title "master wallower", particularly during the warm summer months. In areas where warthogs are common, most trees around a wallow bear the mud smears left by them.

Many species "dry-rub" and their hair may be left on rough bark; cattle had left hair on the bark of this tree. It is possible to identify a species from hair samples but microscopic examination is usually required.

Another form of mud-rubbing is undertaken by the males of a number of antelope species, in which the horns and the face are rubbed in mud as well as dry ground. This can serve as pure display, or in some species as scent-marking from facial glands. Among others, "horning" is undertaken by greater kudu, blue wildebeest, red hartebeest and nyala.

A nyala bull "horning". It is not usually possible to identify the species from the marks left by this habit, except in conjunction with tracks.

Once urine has dried it usually leaves very little sign. There are a few exceptions, such as the white and dark brown streaks left by hyrax urine (see under droppings) on rocks, closely associated with accumulations of their dung pellets. A person with considerable field experience can identify some species from their body or gland scents, for example waterbuck, buffalo, elephant, the large cats, genets and the striped polecat (zorilla).

The large cats make use of urine, combined with scratching by the hind feet, to mark territories and home ranges. These urine-scratches, if fresh, give off a pungent smell and the scratches are clearly visible. This is a leopard urine-scratch on a jeep track; the urine had been squirted on the grass clump.

In this case a gemsbok had urinated on sand and it served to consolidate the urine-soaked area. The loose sand then blew away, leaving a "urine table". These are common in the sand dunes of the Namib Desert. Gerbils frequently use these dried urine patches as the starting point when excavating their burrows.

A bull white rhino spraying urine as a marker. This type of urine marking leaves little sign once it has dried out.

Tree scratching

This is usually associated with the cat family, including the domestic cat. The principal reason for tree scratching is to loosen the outer horny layers of the claws to ensure that they are always sharp. Tree scratching may also play some role in territorial marking in some species. Old claw fragments may be found below these scratching trees. Obviously the clawing of the large cats is more easily found but even then a sharp eye is required. Certain trees may be favoured over others and are frequently used.

Fresh claw marks made by a leopard; note the old, grey claw marks below and to the left of the fresh clawings. In an area of the Soutpansberg (South Africa) we located 19 leopard scratching trees and all were waterberries (Syzygium cordatum), *although many other species were growing in the area.*

Fresh and old leopard tree scratchings.

Numerous fresh and old leopard scratchings; the patches are where bark has been freshly removed by a bushpig – apparently a rare occurrence.

Rolling

Rolling in soft soil or sand is common behaviour in many mammals and dust-bathing is frequent in many bird species. This may take place at any suitable site, which may be used regularly, resulting in distinct hollows. Several species may make use of the same hollow and a confusing array of tracks could be present. In the Namib Desert, for example, Hartmann's zebras frequently create rolling sites in old ostrich nesting depressions.

A roll site used by a plains zebra. This species rolls frequently, as do horses, donkeys and other zebra species.

A roll site used by Hartmann's zebra and gemsbok. Favoured rolling hollows are often located in riverbeds or on floodplains.

This Cape mountain zebra site is next to a yellow mongoose warren where the soil had been loosened and is more suitable for rolling than the surrounding grass-covered earth. We have found Hartmann's zebra roll sites associated with ground squirrel warrens in the Namib Desert.

267

A roll site and lying-up hollow used over a long period by a bull gemsbok; note the numerous dung pellets.

Hyraxes are keen dust-bathers and numerous small hollows (roughly 30 cm in diameter) are located close to their rock shelters.

Many gamebirds use dusting hollows regularly, such as these created by Cape francolin. Characteristic tracks can often be seen, and the vigorous bathing loosens feathers that catch in adjacent vegetation.

Scent-marking

This is a method used by numerous mammals to "signpost" their presence in a home range, either to warn off or attract other members of the same species. Animals use droppings and urine for this purpose; in addition many species have glands that produce secretions which they paste on rocks, twigs, leaves or the soil. Unfortunately, most of these scent-marks are easily overlooked.

268

Many antelope species have glands on the face that produce small quantities of dark secretion to act as "notice-boards" for other members of the same species. Usually a twig tip or firm grass stalk is stuck into the gland and so coated with a dark, tar-like substance. These marking points are often used over long periods of time. Here a klipspringer ewe is marking a twig. The marks are usually associated with large accumulations of dung pellets.

The tip of a twig with an accumulation of klipspringer gland secretion.

The three species of hyaena and the aardwolf paste grass stalks with secretions from their anal glands but only the brown hyaena deposits two distinct secretions on the same grass stalk; this can be clearly seen in the photograph. Only the very observant are likely to find this type of sign. The pastings may be found throughout the home range.

Holes

Holes are excavated by many animals for shelter and by some when feeding (for example the aardvark and porcupine), but there are other reasons for digging into the earth. During dry periods surface water dries up and animals are forced to move to where it is available, or to excavate to sub-surface water. Underground water is usually closest to the surface in riverbeds. Some species also dig to gain access to mineral-rich soils.

This hole in a sandy riverbed was dug by gemsbok but later deepened by savanna baboons. Large numbers of small birds and insects make use of these water sources.

These holes had been opened by Hartmann's zebra but were also used by gemsbok, springbok and black-backed jackal.

Mineral-rich soil exposed by elephant; note the tracks and broken-down dung in the background. Such sites are often exploited for many years, even centuries.

Bark-stripping

This is usually associated with feeding by such species as elephant. We have observed both species of rhinoceros, the buffalo and eland using their horns to strip bark and gouge the wood but eating nothing. Eland and greater kudu bulls use their horns to break off branches to gain access to leaves normally out of reach.

270

A white rhino bull vigorously attacked this tree with its front horn and the higher, older stripped bark indicates that this was not an isolated incident.

Another form of stripping is carried out by members of the weaver family: strips of vegetation are used for nest building and suitable leaves, grasses and reeds are stripped, leaving the plants with a ragged appearance. As I write this, I am looking out at male Cape weavers stripping a once superb specimen of lemon grass.

Grass stripped by lesser masked weavers for nest building.

Hair

As previously mentioned, hair can be identified by microscopic examination. In cases where this is considered important, for example to identify a predator or locate a rare species, good places to collect hair samples are on rough bark, barbed wire or thorns. There are people in conservation or game departments, universities and museums who would be able to assist in identification.

Hair left by a grey rhebok when jumping over a barbed wire. We could identify the species from tracks and confirmed it by checking scale patterns on the hair.

Shed skin

Many invertebrates and reptiles shed their skins in such a way that they are easily found: insects, arachnids and snakes shed the skin in one piece. The shed skins of spiders are probably most familiar as they are commonly found in houses. Because these skins are so complete it is often possible for an expert to identify the species. In the case of snakes the scalation can also aid identification. Although lizards also shed their skins these are usually fragmented and in some cases eaten.

The sloughed skin of a snake. In sheltered sites these skins may remain intact for months.

The shed skin of a cicada nymph: the adult had emerged through a slit in the back. In this case a small spider has taken up residence in the skin.

272

Feathers

Birds drop feathers during preening and moulting, and in attacks by predators. Several thousand species of bird occur in sub-Saharan Africa so it is far beyond the scope of this book to give an identification key. The following photographs are of but a few of the feathers we have collected in our wanderings. If you are particularly interested in identifying any feathers you collect make contact with ornithologists in museums with bird skin collections. Obviously some will be easier to identify than others, so don't expect miracles.

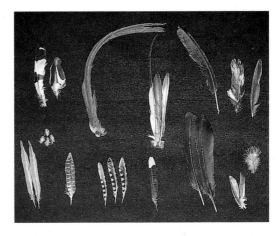

Clockwise from top left: hoopoe, paradise flycatcher, lilacbreasted roller, purplecrested lourie (turaco), glossy starling, Narina trogon, spottedbacked weaver, Knysna lourie, bokmakierie, cardinal woodpecker, ground woodpecker, European bee-eater, redbilled quelea.

Clockwise from top left: black eagle, spotted eagle owl, barn owl, pale chanting goshawk, rufouscheeked nightjar, freckled nightjar, pearlspotted owl, lesser kestrel, rock kestrel.

Clockwise from top left: spotted dikkop, redwinged francolin, Cape francolin, Swainson's francolin, yellowbilled duck, Cape turtle dove, helmeted guineafowl, rock (speckled) pigeon.

Debris

Tracks are frequently left by wind-blown vegetation and other debris and this can be very confusing. We have selected four examples but you should always bear in mind that these tracks can present themselves in many different ways. Wherever possible follow an unfamiliar trail to its end point.

Neat, circular tracks are often made around grass tussocks by bent leaves or stems. By the time the circle is encountered the stalk that had drawn it in the sand has often broken off and been blown away, leaving little indication of the cause of the track.

274

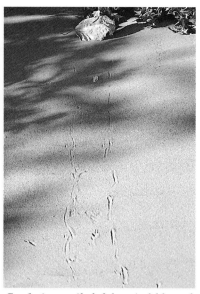

Confusing trails left by wind-blown leaves. A short follow-up will usually reveal the leaf or debris caught against other vegetation, among rocks or in a sheltered hollow.

Water-carried debris, such as pieces of wood, often leave confusing trails on beaches, mud flats and tidal estuaries, and along rivers in receding flood.

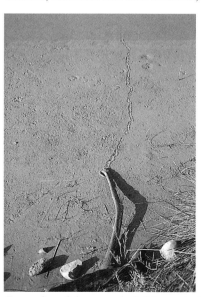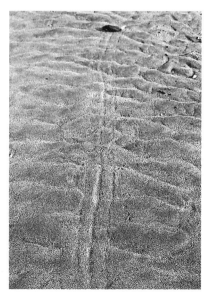

Examples of drag marks left by waterlogged wood in a tidal estuary.

Small circular indentations in sand left by water dripping from vegetation after heavy fog. Note the hyrax tracks in the foreground.

To end this chapter, two photographs of animal signs that are seasonal.

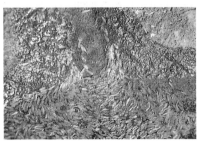

At the beginning of the rainy season many species of termite and ant release large numbers of virgin queens and males to form new colonies. These insects have wings that carry them a short distance from the mother-colony. However, the wings are soon shed and may form large accumulations. They are particularly noticeable if they fall into pools of water.

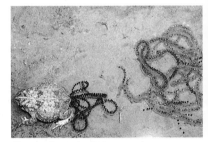

Frogs deposit their eggs in many different situations but those of the toads are laid in long strings of jelly in shallow, still water. This is a female Karoo toad laying egg-strings.

8 SKULLS

Skulls and bones are not only interesting objects in their own right but they are frequently encountered and can provide you with a wealth of information. Skulls can provide proof of a species' presence in an area, and bones and skulls in owl pellets can be used to determine the owl's diet and the abundance of its prey. We have selected a few examples of the skulls of the major mammal groups. A brief description is given with each similar group of skulls, as well as the average total skull length of the species. However, if you find a skull and require an accurate identification, take the specimen to your closest natural history museum.

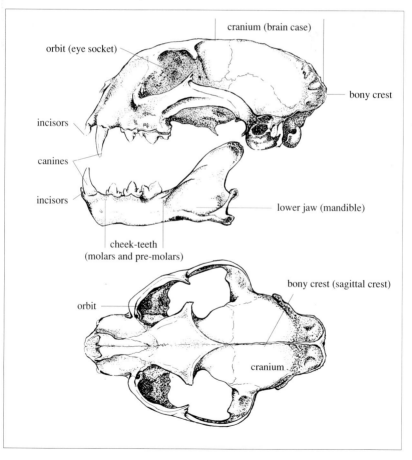

A word of warning: Some of the skulls and bones you find on your wanderings may have belonged to animals that had died of potentially harmful diseases, such as rabies and anthrax, so be careful when handling them.

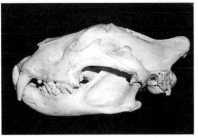

The cats have large canines and the cheek-teeth are sharp-edged for cutting; a prominent crest on the top of the cranium may be present. This is the skull of a lion (40 cm).

Leopard (22 cm).

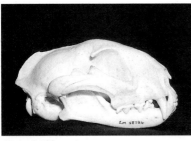

Serval (12 cm).

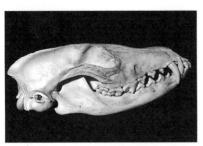

Side-striped jackal (17 cm). Note the more slender canines in this species.

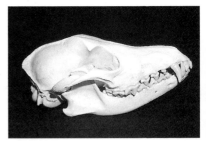

The dogs have fairly large canines but they are somewhat smaller than those of the cats, with the exception of the wild dog. All dog species have more teeth than the cats (at least 10 more but this varies according to species). A low crest may be present on the cranium. This is the skull of a black-backed jackal (17 cm).

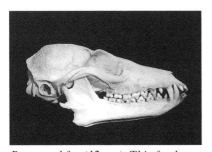

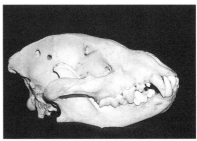

Bat-eared fox (12 cm). This fox has a massive total of 46 teeth. The cheek-teeth do not have well-developed cutting edges but are suited to grinding insects which form the bulk of the fox's diet.

The three hyaena species have massive teeth, heavy skulls and a well-developed crest on the cranium. The impressive teeth can crush even heavy leg bones. A hyaena skull could be confused with that of the more lightly built wild dog, but the skull of this endangered species is unlikely to be encountered. This is a spotted hyaena skull (28 cm).

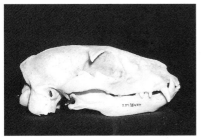

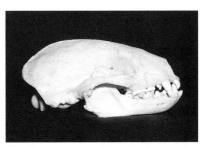

The aardwolf is sometimes placed with the hyaenas but it has a dramatically different skull structure. Although the canines are well developed the few cheek-teeth are tiny pegs and the skull is light. As this animal feeds almost exclusively on termites it has no need for large teeth or a heavy bone structure. This aardwolf skull is 14 cm.

The honey badger has a heavy skull (15 cm) and powerful teeth.

279

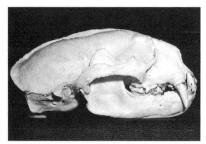
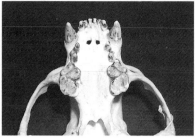

The two species of clawless otter have heavy, broad skulls with well-developed canines and massive, flattened cheek-teeth that are used to crush hard prey such as crabs. A low crest is usually present on the cranium. This is the skull of a Congo clawless otter (15 cm).

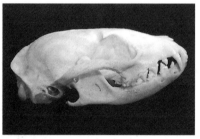
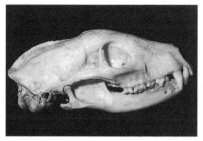

The genets and the mongooses are included in the large group of small carnivores known as viverrids. They are all superficially similar, most with light skulls and fairly small teeth, and are difficult to separate by the non-expert. This is the skull of a large-spotted genet (9 cm).

White-tailed mongoose (11 cm). Note the well-developed crest on the cranium.

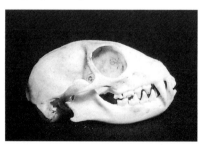

Suricate (6,5 cm). Note the large eye socket.

Banded mongoose (7 cm).

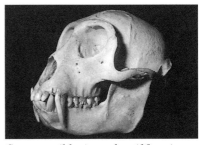

The primates (monkeys, baboons and apes) have distinct skulls with forward-pointing eye sockets, well-developed canines and flattened cheek-teeth for crushing and chewing food. This is the skull of a male savanna baboon (24 cm); those of females are shorter.

Samango (blue) monkey (10 cm).

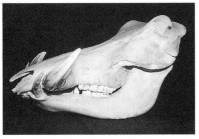

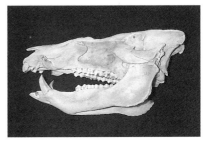

The warthog has a heavy skull with large "tusks" (tushes); these are particularly well developed in boars. The cheek-teeth are flattened for chewing. Skull length is 40 cm.

The bushpig has a heavy skull (38 cm) but the tushes are much smaller than those of the warthog.

Hippos have very large tusk-like canines and incisors and the cheek-teeth are flattened. Skull length is 65 cm.

The skulls of the two rhinoceros species are massive and heavy, with very large, flattened cheek-teeth. There is a knob of raised bone on the "nose tip". The skull of the white rhino (76 cm) is much longer than that of the black rhino (55 cm).

The skull of a steenbok ewe (14 cm). The females of some antelope species bear horns but these are usually lighter than those of the males. All antelope have incisor teeth at the point of the lower jaw but there are never any on the upper jaw. This also applies to cattle, the buffalo, sheep, goats and the giraffe.

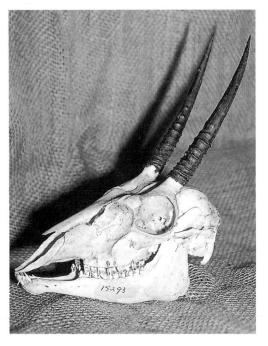

The males of all antelope species bear horns and an identification can be based on horn form and structure. Antelope skulls are fairly light and the cheek-teeth have broad surfaces for grinding their plant food. Because of the great number of species occurring in Africa we have decided to include only two examples here. Antelope skulls can be identified from mammal field guides that are available. This skull is of an oribi ram.

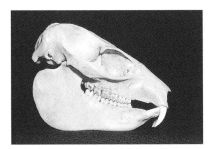

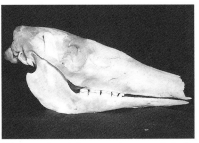

The hyraxes occur widely and their skulls are commonly found. The upper incisors are well developed and they are tusk-like in appearance. Those of the males are triangular in cross-section and those of the females rounded on their front surface. The cheek-teeth resemble those of other herbivores. This skull is of a tree hyrax (9 cm).

The aardvark has an elongated skull and the flat cheek-teeth are ideally suited to crushing its termite prey. The skull of this animal (20 cm) is rarely found – we have collected only two in 18 years.

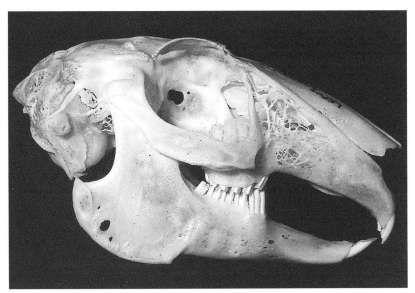

The hares and rabbits have similar skulls: they are very light and in front of the eye sockets the bone is particularly thin and has a lace-like appearance. The incisors are like those of the rodents but not as robust. This is the skull of a scrub hare (10 cm; all other species are smaller).

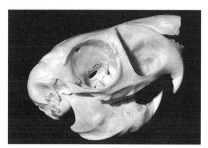

The rodents range greatly in size but all species have two pairs of very well developed incisors and the cheek-teeth are adapted for grinding and crushing food. This is the skull of a springhare (8,5 cm). Note the very large eye socket.

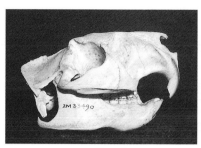

Greater canerat (8 cm).

The porcupine has a large, rounded cranium, massive incisors and very small eye sockets. Skull length is 14 cm.

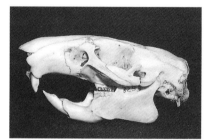

Giant rat (7 cm).

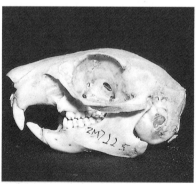

Southern ground squirrel (6 cm).

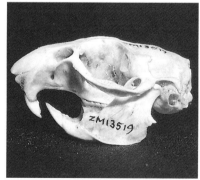

Vlei rat (3,5 cm).

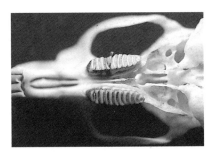

Note the "laminated" structure of the cheek-teeth of a vlei rat. This is characteristic of all species of Otomys *and* Parotomys. *Their skulls are commonly found in owl pellets, particularly those of the barn owl.*

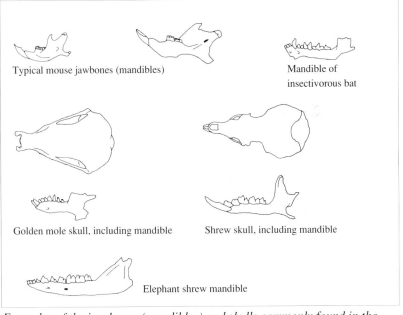

Typical mouse jawbones (mandibles)

Mandible of insectivorous bat

Golden mole skull, including mandible

Shrew skull, including mandible

Elephant shrew mandible

Examples of the jaw bones (mandibles) and skulls commonly found in the regurgitated pellets of the barn owl and the eagle owls.

The elephant shrews have light, delicate skulls and these are often found in owl pellets. This is the skull of a chequered elephant shrew (7 cm; most species are considerably smaller).

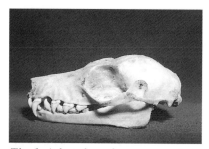

The fruit bats have large eye sockets and light skulls. This is of a Wahlberg's epaulletted fruit bat (4,2 cm).

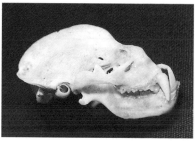

Most of the insect-eating bats have tiny skulls (1-2 cm), with an array of impressively needle-sharp teeth, notably the canines. This is of a Commerson's leaf-nosed bat (3,2 cm).

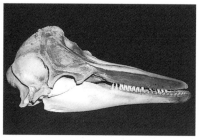

Dolphins and other small cetaceans occasionally get stranded on our beaches and their skulls may be found. The structure is variable. This is the skull of a bottle-nosed dolphin (55 cm).

The Nile crocodile (two other species occur in equatorial Africa) has been greatly reduced in numbers and skulls are seldom found, but we occasionally stumble across them.

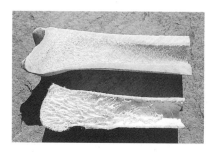

The bones of birds and mammals differ in that bird bones are much lighter and the internal structure is less cluttered. The internal network of mammal bones is very dense, hence the greater mass. At top is a mammal bone (horse), below it a bird bone (ostrich).

9 APPENDICES

GLOSSARY

ANTERIOR: The front.

CALCIUM: An alkaline, silvery-white metallic element found, for example, in animal bones.

CANINES: The teeth (two in each jaw) situated between the incisors and the premolars.

CARAPACE: Hard structure covering all or part of an animal's body, for example the upper part of a tortoise shell.

CARNIVORE: Flesh-eating mammal.

CHEEK-TEETH: The teeth (molars and premolars) that lie behind the canines.

CLOACA: Single chamber into which digestive, urinary and reproductive systems empty their contents; it has only one external opening.

CLOVEN HOOF: The divided hoof of pigs, goats, cattle, antelope, etc.

COAGULATE: To change from a fluid into a soft, semi-solid mass.

COLONIAL: Describes animals that live in groups, such as colonial-nesting birds and certain small mammals.

CORM: Underground storage and reproductive structure of certain plants formed by swelling of the stem; bulbs are formed by swelling of leaf bases.

CRANIUM: The part of the skull that encloses the brain.

DECOMPOSE: To break down, or be broken down, into constituent elements by bacterial or fungal action (to rot).

DREY: Domed nest constructed with leaves and twigs, usually by tree-dwelling squirrels.

ELYTRA: The modified fore-wings of beetles that are usually hardened and act as protective cover for the soft body.

HABITAT: The place where an organism (animal or plant) or population normally lives.

HERBIVORE: An animal that feeds principally on plants. Grazers feed mainly on grasses and browsers mainly on woody or herbaceous plants.

HOLT: Shelter used by otters.

HOME RANGE: The area used by an animal during the course of its day-to-day activities.

HUMUS: Partially decomposed organic matter in the soil.

INCISORS: Sharp-edged front teeth, usually in both the upper and lower jaws. The giraffe, cattle, sheep, goats and antelope have incisors on only the lower jaw.

INSECTIVOROUS: Animals (usually referring to mammals and birds) that feed mainly on insects.

LATRINE SITE: A small area in which an individual, or several animals of the same species, deposit the faeces (droppings).

MIDDEN: An accumulation of inedible food remains, collected together in a small area by such species as black-backed jackal and brown hyaena.

OESOPHAGUS: The part of the digestive tract between the pharynx and the stomach.

POSTERIOR: The rear or back.

PREORBITAL GLAND: A gland located in front of the eye.

PRIMATES: Any mammal of the order Primates, including humans, bushbabies, monkeys and baboons.

RAPTOR: A bird of prey.

REGURGITATE: To expel through the mouth undigested food remains, or partly digested food.

ROOST: A location where birds and bats rest or sleep.

RUT: A period of sexual excitement and reproductive activity in certain male ruminants.

SCAPULA: The shoulder blade.

SCAVENGERS: Animals that feed on dead or decaying organic matter.

SECRETION: A substance that is released from a cell. In the animal world these substances are commonly used for marking an animal's living space and provides information on such aspects as sexual condition.

SLOUGH: To shed the skin, like snakes and lizards do.

SPRAINT: Small amount of faeces (droppings) deposited by an otter for marking purposes.

SQUAB: Young unfledged bird, especially pigeons and doves.

STERNUM: Breast bone.

SUBSTRATE: Underlying layer.

TERRITORY: A restricted area occupied by an animal, usually for breeding purposes, and actively defended from other individuals of the same species.

WARREN: A series of interconnected underground tunnels in which some burrowing mammals live.

FURTHER READING

BOYCOTT, R.C. & BORQUIN, D. 1988. *The South African Tortoise Book: a Guide to Southern African Tortoises.* Southern Book Publishers, Johannesburg.

BRANCH, W. 1988. *Field Guide to the Snakes and Other Reptiles of Southern Africa.* Struik Publishers, Cape Town.

BROADLEY, D.G. 1983. *FitzSimon's Snakes of Southern Africa.* Delta Books, Johannesburg.

FILMER, M.R. 1991. *Southern African Spiders: an Identification Guide.* Struik Publishers, Cape Town.

HALTENORTH, T. & DILLER, H. 1984. *A Field Guide to the Mammals of Africa Including Madagascar.* Collins, London.

KINGDON, J. 1971-1982. *East African Mammals: an Atlas of Evolution in Africa.* (Vols I-III). Academic Press, London.

LIEBENBERG, L. 1990. *A Field Guide to the Animal Tracks of Southern Africa.* David Philip Publishers, Cape Town.

MACLEAN, G.L. 1993. *Roberts' Birds of Southern Africa.* The Trustees of the John Voelcker Bird Book Fund, Cape Town.

NEWMAN, K.B. 1992. *Newman's Birds of Southern Africa.* Southern Book Publishers, Johannesburg.

SKAIFE, F.H. 1987. *African Insect Life.* Struik Publishers, Cape Town.

SKINNER, J. & SMITHERS, R.H.N. 1990. *The Mammals of the Southern African Subregion.* University of Pretoria, Pretoria.

STUART, C. & STUART, T. 1992. *Field Guide to the Mammals of Southern Africa.* Struik Publishers, Cape Town.

STUART, C. & STUART, T. 1992. *Southern, Central and East African Mammals: a Photographic Guide.* Struik Publishers, Cape Town.

WILLIAMS, J.G. & ARLOTT, N. 1992. *Field Guide: Birds of East Africa.* Collins, London.

DISTRIBUTION AND HABITAT CHECK LIST

	Transvaal (SA)	Natal (SA)	Orange Free State (SA)	Cape (SA)	Namibia	Botswana	Zimbabwe	Mozambique	Zambia	Angola	Malawi	Zaïre	Tanzania	Kenya	Uganda	Arid	Wetland	Forest	Woodland	Savanna
Aardvark	★	★	★	★	★	★	★	★	★	★	★	★	★	★	★	★			★	★
Aardwolf	★	★	★	★	★	★	★	★	★	★			★	★	★	★			★	★
Antelope royal	★											★			★			★		
Badger, honey	★	★	★	★	★	★	★	★	★	★	★	★	★	★	★	★			★	★
Baboon, savanna	★	★	★	★	★	★	★	★	★	★	★	★	★	★	★	★	★	★	★	★
Bontebok/Blesbok	★	★	★	★																★
Bongo												★		★				★		
Bonobo												★						★		
Buffalo	★	★	★	★	★	★	★	★	★	★	★	★	★	★	★		★	★	★	★
Bushbaby (greater)	★	★				★	★	★	★	★	★	★	★	★					★	★
Bushbaby (other)	★			★	★	★	★	★	★	★	★	★	★	★	★				★	★
Bushbuck	★	★		★	★	★	★	★	★	★	★	★	★	★	★		★	★	★	
Bushpig	★	★		★	★	★	★	★	★	★	★	★	★	★	★		★	★	★	
Canerat	★	★		★	★	★	★	★	★	★	★	★	★	★	★	★				★
Caracal	★	★	★	★	★	★	★	★	★	★	★	★	★	★	★	★		★	★	★
Cat, African wild	★	★	★	★	★	★	★	★	★	★	★	★	★	★	★	★			★	★
Cheetah	★	★		★	★	★	★	★	★	★	★	★	★	★	★	★			★	★
Chimpanzee												★	★		★			★	★	★
Civet	★	★			★	★	★	★	★	★	★	★	★	★	★		★	★	★	★
Dassie, (rock hyrax)	★	★	★	★	★	★	★	★	★	★	★	★	★	★	★	★			★	★
Dassie, (tree hyrax)		★		★				★	★			★	★	★	★			★		
Dik-dik (4 species)					★					★			★	★		★			★	
Dog, wild	★	★			★	★	★	★	★	★	★	★	★	★	★	★			★	★
Duiker, blue		★		★			★	★	★	★	★	★	★	★	★			★	★	
Duiker, common	★	★	★	★	★	★	★	★	★	★	★	★	★	★	★				★	★
Duiker, red	★	★						★	★		★	★	★	★	★			★	★	
Duiker, yellow-backed									★	★		★	★	★	★			★	★	
Eland	★	★	★	★	★	★	★	★	★	★	★	★	★	★	★	★			★	★
Elephant	★	★		★	★	★	★	★	★	★	★	★	★	★	★	★	★	★	★	★
Elephant shrew	★	★	★	★	★	★	★	★	★	★	★	★	★	★	★	★			★	★
Fox, bat-eared	★		★	★	★	★	★	★			★		★	★	★	★				★
Fox, Cape	★	★	★	★	★	★					★				★					★
Gazelle, Grant's													★	★	★	★				★
Gazelle, Thomson's													★	★						★
Gemsbok, (oryx)	★			★	★	★	★			★			★	★	★	★				★
Genet	★	★	★	★	★	★	★	★	★	★	★	★	★	★	★	★	★	★	★	★
Gerbil, *Gerbillurus*	★	★	★	★	★	★	★	★		★					★				★	★
Gerbil, *Tatera*	★	★	★	★	★	★	★	★	★	★	★	★	★	★	★				★	★
Gerenuk													★	★		★				★
Giraffe	★	★			★	★	★	★	★	★		★	★	★	★	★			★	★
Gorilla										★		★			★			★		
Grysbok, Cape				★															★	
Grysbok, Sharpe's	★					★	★	★	★		★	★	★							★
Hare, Cape	★		★	★	★	★	★	★		★			★	★	★	★				★
Hare, scrub	★	★	★	★	★	★	★	★	★	★	★	★	★	★	★	★			★	★
Hartebeest, red (bubal)	★			★	★	★				★		★	★	★	★				★	★
Hedgehog	★		★	★	★	★	★	★	★	★		★	★	★	★				★	★
Hippopotamus	★	★		★	★	★	★	★	★	★	★	★	★	★	★		★			
Hog, giant forest												★	★	★	★			★		
Hyaena, brown	★	★	★	★	★	★	★	★		★				★					★	★
Hyaena, spotted	★	★		★	★	★	★	★	★	★	★	★	★	★	★				★	★
Hyaena, striped													★	★		★			★	★
Impala	★	★			★	★	★	★	★	★	★	★	★	★	★				★	★
Jackal, black-backed	★	★	★	★	★	★	★	★		★			★	★	★	★			★	★
Jackal, golden												★	★	★	★	★			★	★
Jackal, side-striped	★	★			★	★	★	★	★	★	★	★	★	★	★			★	★	★

	Transvaal (SA)	Natal (SA)	Orange Free State (SA)	Cape (SA)	Namibia	Botswana	Zimbabwe	Mozambique	Zambia	Angola	Malawi	Zaïre	Tanzania	Kenya	Uganda	Arid	Wetland	Forest	Woodland	Savanna
Klipspringer	★	★	★	★	★	★	★	★	★	★	★	★	★	★	★	★	★			★
Kob												★		★			★			★
Kudu, greater	★	★	★	★	★	★	★	★	★	★	★	★	★	★	★	★			★	★
Kudu, Lesser												★	★	★	★	★			★	★
Lechwe					★	★			★								★			
Leopard	★	★		★	★	★	★	★	★	★	★	★	★	★	★	★	★	★	★	★
Lion	★	★		★	★	★	★	★	★	★	★	★	★	★	★	★			★	★
Mole, golden	★	★	★	★	★		★	★	★	★		★	★	★	★	★		★	★	★
Mongoose, banded	★	★				★	★	★	★	★	★	★	★	★	★				★	★
Mongoose, dwarf	★	★		★	★	★	★		★	★	★	★	★	★	★				★	★
Mongoose, large grey	★	★		★	★	★	★	★	★	★	★	★	★	★	★		★	★	★	★
Mongoose, slender	★	★	★	★	★	★	★	★	★	★	★	★	★	★	★	★	★		★	★
Mongoose, small grey	★	★	★	★	★					★						★			★	★
Mongoose, water	★	★	★	★		★	★	★	★	★	★	★	★	★	★		★			★
Mongoose, white-tailed	★	★	★	★	★	★	★	★	★	★	★	★	★	★	★		★		★	★
Mongoose, yellow	★	★	★	★	★	★	★			★					★					★
Monkey, vervet	★	★	★	★	★	★	★	★	★	★	★	★	★	★	★	★			★	★
Nyala	★	★					★	★			★								★	
Okapi												★						★		
Oribi	★	★	★	★	★	★	★	★	★	★	★	★	★	★	★					★
Otter, clawless	★	★	★	★	★	★	★	★	★	★	★	★	★	★	★		★			
Otter, spotted-necked	★	★	★	★	★	★		★	★	★	★	★	★	★	★		★			
Porcupine	★	★	★	★	★	★	★	★	★	★	★	★	★	★	★	★		★	★	★
Puku						★			★	★	★	★	★				★			
Rabbit, red rock	★	★	★	★	★	★	★	★	★	★		★	★	★	★					★
Rat, Otomys	★	★	★	★	★	★	★	★	★	★	★	★	★	★	★	★		★	★	★
Reedbuck, bohor												★	★	★	★		★			★
Reedbuck, mountain	★	★	★	★		★						★	★						★	★
Reedbuck, southern	★	★				★	★	★	★	★	★	★		★			★			★
Rhebok, grey	★	★	★	★												★				★
Rhino, black	★	★		★	★		★	★	★	★	★		★	★		★			★	★
Rhino, white	★	★	★	★	★	★	★				★	★		★					★	★
Roan	★				★	★	★	★	★	★	★	★	★	★	★				★	★
Rodent molerats	★	★	★	★	★	★	★	★	★	★	★	★	★	★	★	★			★	★
Root rat												★	★	★	★			★	★	
Sable												★		★				★		
Serval	★	★	★		★	★	★	★	★	★	★	★	★	★	★	★		★	★	★
Shrew	★	★	★	★	★	★	★	★	★	★	★	★	★	★	★	★	★	★	★	★
Sitatunga					★	★			★	★		★	★	★	★		★			
Springbok	★		★	★	★	★				★						★				★
Springhare	★	★	★	★	★	★	★	★	★	★			★	★	★	★			★	★
Squirrel, ground	★		★	★	★	★				★			★	★	★	★				★
Steenbok	★	★	★		★	★	★	★	★	★			★	★		★				★
Suni	★	★					★	★			★		★	★					★	
Suricate	★	★	★		★	★	★			★						★				★
Tsessebe/Topi	★					★	★	★			★		★	★	★				★	★
Warthog	★	★		★	★	★	★	★	★	★	★	★	★	★	★				★	★
Waterbuck	★	★				★	★	★	★	★	★	★	★	★	★		★		★	★
Weasel, striped	★	★	★	★	★	★	★	★	★	★	★	★	★		★					★
Wildebeest, black	★	★	★	★																★
Wildebeest, blue	★	★		★	★	★	★	★	★	★		★	★						★	★
Zebra, Grevy's													★		★					★
Zebra, Hartmann's				★	★					★						★				★
Zebra, plains	★	★			★	★	★	★	★	★	★	★	★	★	★				★	★
Zebra, mountain				★																★
Zorilla	★	★	★	★	★	★	★	★	★	★	★	★	★	★	★			★	★	★

MAMMAL LIST

English common names have been used throughout the text, you can use this list to find the scientific name (in italic), Afrikaans, German and French (where they exist) names for the mammals mentioned in the text.

Aardwolf □ *Proteles cristatus* □ Aardwolf □ Erdwolf □ Protèle
Antbear(Aardvark) □ *Orycteropus afer* □ Erdvark □ Erdferkel □ Oryctérope

Baboon, savanna (chacma,yellow,olive) □ *Papio cynocephalus(ursinus)* □ Bobbejaan □
     Steppenpavian(Tschakmapavian,Gelber P.,Anubispavian) □ Babouin(Chacma)
Bat, Cape serotine □ *Eptesicus capensis* □ Kaapse dakvlermuis □ Kap–Breitflügelfledermaus □
     Sérotine du Cap
Bat, Commerson's leaf–nosed □ *Hipposideros commersoni* □ Commerson–bladneusvlermuis □
     Commerson–Rundblattnase/Riesen-Rundblattnase □ Phyllorine de Commerson
Bat, Egyptian slit–faced □ *Nycteris thebaica* □ Egiptiese spleetneusvlermuis □
     Ägyptische Schlitznase(nfledermaus) □ Nyctère de Geoffroy
Blesbok/Bontebok □ *Damaliscus dorcas* □ Blesbok/Bontebok □ Blesbock/Buntebock □
     Blesbok/Bontebok
Bongo □ *Boocercus euryceros* □ Bongo □ Bongo □ Bongo
Bonobo □ *Pan paniscus* □ Bonobo □ Bonobo □ Chimpanzé nain
Buffalo □ *Syncerus caffer* □ Buffel □ Büffel □ Buffle d'Afrique
Bushbaby, lesser □ *Galago moholi* □ Nagapie □ Kleiner Galago □ Galago du Sénégal
Bushbaby, thick–tailed □ *Otolemur crassicaudatus* □ Bosnagaap □ Riesengalago □
     Galago à queue épaisse
Bushbuck □ *Tragelaphus scriptus* □ Bosbok □ Buschbock □ Guib harnaché
Bushpig □ *Potamochoerus porcus* □ Bosvark □ Buschschwein □ Potamochère

Camel □ *Camelus dromedarius* □ Kameel □ Dromedar □ Chameau
Canerat, greater □ *Thryonomys swinderianus* □ Grootrietrot □ Große Rohrratte □ Aulacode grand
Caracal □ *Felis caracal* □ Rooikat □ Karakal(Wüstenluchs) □ Caracal
Cat, African wild □ *Felis libyca* □ Vaalboskat □ Afrikanische Falbkatze □ Chat sauvage d'Afrique
Cat, domestic □ *Felis catus* □ Huiskat □ Hauskatze □ Chat
Cat, golden □ *Felis aurata* □ Gouekat □ Afrikanische Goldkatze □ Chat doré
Cat, small–spotted □ *Felis nigripes* □ Swartpootkat □ Schwarzfußkatze □ Chat à pieds noirs
Cattle, domestic □ *Bos taurus* □ Bees □ Hausrind □ Bœuf
Cheetah □ *Acinonyx jubatus* □ Jagluiperd □ Gepard □ Guépard
Chimpanzee □ *Pan troglodytes* □ Sjimpansee □ Schimpanse □ Chimpanzé
Civet, African □ *Civettictis civetta* □ Siwet □ Afrikanische Zibetkatze □ Civette

Dassierat □ *Petromus typicus* □ Dassierot □ Felsenratte □ Rat typique (de rochers)
Dik–dik, Kirk's (Damara) □ *Madoqua kirkii* □ Damara–dikdik □ Kirkdikdik (Kirk–Dik–Dik) □
     Dik–dik de Kirk
Dog, wild □ *Lycaon pictus* □ Wildehond □ Afrikanischer Wildhund □ Lycaon/Cynhyène
Dolphin, bottle–nosed □ *Tursiops truncatus* □ Stompneusdolfyn □ Großer Tümmler □ Souffleur
Donkey, domestic □ *Equus asinus* □ Donkie □ Esel □ Âne
Dormouse, spectacled □ *Graphiurus ocularis* □ Gemsbokmuis □ Brillenbilch □ Graphiure
Duiker, blue □ *Philantomba monticola* □ Blouduiker □ Blauducker □ Céphalophe bleu
Duiker, common □ *Sylvicapra grimmia* □ Gewone duiker □ Kronenducker □ Céphalophe de Grimm
Duiker, red □ *Cephalophus natalensis* □ Rooiduiker □ Rotducker □ Céphalophe du Natal

Eland □ *Taurotragus oryx* □ Eland □ Elenantilope □ Eland du Cap
Elephant □ *Loxodonta africana* □ Olifant □ Elefant □ Eléphant d'Afrique
Elephant shrew, chequered □ *Rhynchocyon cirnei* □ Reuse klaasneus □ Geflecktes Rüsselhündchen

Forest hog, giant □ *Hylochoerus meinertzhageni* □ Reuse bosvark □ Riesenwaldschwein □ Hylochère
Fox, bat–eared □ *Otocyon megalotis* □ Bakoorjakkals □ Löffelhund □ Otocyon
Fox, Cape □ *Vulpes chama* □ Silwervos □ Kapfuchs □ Renard du Cap
Fruit–bat, Wahlberg's epaulletted □ *Epomorphus wahlbergi* □ Wahlberg–witkolvrugtevlermuis □
        Wahlberg–Epaulettenflughund □ Épomophore de Wahlberg

Gazelle, Grant's □ *Gazella granti* □ Grant–gazelle □ Grant–Gazelle □ Gazelle de Grant
Gazelle, Thomson's □ *Gazella thomsoni* □ Thomson–gazelle □ Thomson–Gazelle □ Gazelle de Thomson
Genet, large–spotted □ *Genetta tigrina* □ Grootkolmuskejaatkat □ Großfleckginsterkatze □
        Genette tigrine
Genet, small–spotted □ *Genetta genetta* □ Kleinkolmuskejaatkat □ Kleinfleckginsterkatze □
        Genette commune
Gerbil, brush–tailed hairy–footed □ *Gerbillurus vallinus* □ Borselstert–haarpootnagmuis
Gerbil, Cape □ *Tatera afra* □ Kaapse nagmuis □ Kap–Nacktsohlenrennmaus □ Gerboise du Cap
Gerbil, hairy–footed □ *Gerbillurus paeba* □ Haarpootnagmuis □
        Haarsohlenrennmaus(Südafrikan.Zwergrennmaus)
Gerenuk □ *Litocranius walleri* □ Gerenuk □ Giraffengazelle □ Gazelle–girafe
Giraffe □ *Giraffa camelopardalis* □ Kameelperd □ Giraffe □ Girafe
Goat, domestic □ *Capra aegagrus hircus* □ Bok □ Hausziege □ Chèvre
Golden mole, Grant's □ *Eremitalpa granti* □ Grant–gouemol □ Grant–Goldmull/Wüstengoldmull □
        Taupe dorée de Grant
Golden mole, Hottentot □ *Amblysomus hottentotus* □ Hottentot–gouemol □ Hottentotten–Goldmull
Gorilla □ *Gorilla gorilla* □ Gorilla □ Gorilla □ Gorille
Grysbok, Cape □ *Raphicerus melanotis* □ Kaapse grysbok □ Kap–Greisbock □ Grysbok
Grysbok, Sharpe's □ *Raphicerus sharpei* □ Sharpe–grysbok □ Sharpe–Greisbock □ Grysbok de Sharpe

Hare, Cape □ *Lepus capensis* □ Vlakhaas □ Kaphase □ Lièvre du Cap
Hartebeest, Lichtenstein's □ *Sigmoceros lichtensteinii* □ Lichtenstein–hartbees □
        Lichtenstein–Kuhantilope □ Bubale de Lichtenstein
Hartebeest, red □ *Alcelaphus buselaphus* □ Rooihartbees □ Rote Kuhantilope □ Bubale
Hedgehog, southern African □ *Atelerix frontalis* □ Suider–Afrikaanse krimpvarkie □
        Südafrikanischer Igel □ Hérisson d'Afrique du Sud
Hedgehog, white–bellied □ *Atelerix albiventris* □ Oost–Afrikaanse krimpvarkie □ Weißbauchigel □
        Hérisson à ventre blanc
Hippopotamus □ *Hippopotamus amphibius* □ Seekoei □ Flußpferd □ Hippopotame
Horse, domestic □ *Equus caballus* □ Perd □ Pferd □ Cheval
Hyaena, brown □ *Hyaena brunnea* □ Strandjut □ Braune Hyäne □ Hyène brune
Hyaena, spotted □ *Crocuta crocuta* □ Gevlekte hiëna □ Fleckenhyäne □ Hyène tachetée
Hyaena, striped □ *Hyaena hyaena* □ Gestreep–hiëna □ Streifenhyäne □ Hyène rayée
Hyrax, rock □ *Procavia capensis* □ Klipdassie □ Klippschliefer/Dassie □ Daman de rocher
Hyrax, tree □ *Dendrohyrax arboreus* □ Boomdassie □ Baumschliefer □ Daman d'arbre

Impala □ *Aepycerus melampus* □ Rooibok □ Impala(Schwarzfersenantilope) □ Impala

Jackal, black–backed □ *Canis mesomelas* □ Rooijakkals □ Schabrackenschakal □ Chacal à chabraque
Jackal, side–striped □ *Canis adustus* □ Witkwasjakkals □ Streifenschakal □ Chacal à flancs rayés

Klipspringer □ *Oreotragus oreotragus* □ Klipspringer □ Klippspringer □ Oréotrague
Kob □ *Kobus kob* □ Poekoe □ Grasantilope(Kob) □ Cobe de Buffon
Kudu, greater □ *Tragelaphus strepsiceros* □ Koedoe □ Großer Kudu □ Grand Koudou
Kudu, lesser □ *Tragelaphus imberbis* □ Kleinkoedoe □ Kleiner Kudu □ Petit Koudou

Lechwe □ *Kobus leche* □ Lechwe □ Litschi(–Moorantilope) □ Cobe lechwe
Leopard □ *Panthera pardus* □ Luiperd □ Leopard □ Léopard
Lion □ *Panthera leo* □ Leeu □ Löwe □ Lion

Molerat, Cape dune □ *Bathyergus suillus* □ Kaapse duinmol □ Kap–Strandgräber □ Fouisseur

Molerat, common ☐ *Cryptomys hottentotus* ☐ Gewone knaagdiermol ☐
      Hottentottenmullratte/Hottentotten–Graumull ☐ Rat–taupe africain
Molerat, Damara ☐ *Cryptomys damarensis* ☐ Damara–knaagdiermol ☐ Damaramullratte
Molerat, naked ☐ *Heterocephalus glaber* ☐ Nakend–knaagdiermol ☐ Nacktmull ☐ Rat nu de sable
Molerat, Cape ☐ *Georychus capensis* ☐ Blesmol ☐ Kap–Bleßmull ☐ Rat–taupe du Cap
Mongoose, banded ☐ *Mungos mungo* ☐ Gebande muishond ☐ Zebramanguste ☐ Mangue rayeé
Mongoose, dwarf ☐ *Helogale parvula* ☐ Dwergmuishond ☐ Zwergmanguste ☐ Mangouste naine
Mongoose, large grey ☐ *Herpestes ichneumon* ☐ Grootgrysmuishond ☐ Ichneumon ☐
      Mangouste ichneumon
Mongoose, slender ☐ *Galerella sanguinea* ☐ Swartkwasmuishond ☐ Schlankichneumon ☐
      Mangouste rouge
Mongoose, small grey ☐ *Galerella pulverulenta* ☐ Kleingrysmuishond ☐ Klein–Ichneumon ☐
      Mangouste grise du Cap
Mongoose, water ☐ *Atilax paludinosus* ☐ Kommetjiegatmuishond ☐ Sumpfmanguste ☐
      Mangouste des marais
Mongoose, white–tailed ☐ *Ichneumia albicauda* ☐ Witstertmuishond ☐ Weißschwanzmanguste ☐
      Mangouste à queue blanche
Mongoose, yellow ☐ *Cynictis penicillata* ☐ Geelmuishond ☐ Fuchsmanguste ☐ Mangouste fauve
Monkey, vervet ☐ *Cercopithecus aethiops* ☐ Blouaap ☐ Grünmeerkatze ☐ Vervet
Monkey, blue (samango) ☐ *Cercopithecus mitis* ☐ Samango–aap ☐ Diademmeerkatze ☐
      Cercopithèque à diadème
Mouse, Cape spiny ☐ *Acomys subspinosus* ☐ Kaapse stekelmuis ☐ Kap–Stachelmaus
Mouse, house ☐ *Mus musculus* ☐ Huismuis ☐ Hausmaus ☐ Souris domestique
Mouse, multimammate ☐ *Praomys natalensis* ☐ Vaalveldmuis ☐ Vielzitzenmaus
Mouse, Namaqua rock ☐ *Aethomys namaquensis* ☐ Namaqua–klipmuis ☐ Felsenmaus
Mouse, striped ☐ *Rhabdomys pumilio* ☐ Streepmuis ☐ Streifengrasmaus ☐ Rat de champ rayé
Mouse, tree ☐ *Thallomys paedulcus* ☐ Boommuis

Nyala ☐ *Tragelaphus angasii* ☐ Njala ☐ Nyala ☐ Nyala

Okapi ☐ *Okapia johnstoni* ☐ Okapi ☐ Okapi ☐ Okapi
Oribi ☐ *Ourebia ourebi* ☐ Oorbietjie ☐ Oribi ☐ Ourébi
Oryx (gemsbok) ☐ *Oryx gazella* ☐ Gemsbok ☐ Oryx(Spießbock) ☐ Oryx
Otter, Cape clawless ☐ *Aonyx capensis* ☐ Kaapse groototter ☐ Kap–Fingerotter ☐ Loutre à joues blanches
Otter, Congo clawless ☐ *Aonyx congica* ☐ Kongo groototter ☐ Kongo–Fingerotter ☐
      Loutre à joues blanches du Congo
Otter, spotted–necked ☐ *Lutra maculicollis* ☐ Kleinotter ☐ Fleckenhalsotter ☐ Loutre à cou tacheté

Polecat, striped ☐ *Ictonyx striatus* ☐ Stinkmuishond ☐ Zorilla ☐ Zorille commun
Porcupine ☐ *Hystrix africaeaustralis* ☐ Ystervark ☐ Stachelschwein ☐ Porc–épic
Puku ☐ *Kobus vardonii* ☐ Poekoe ☐ Puku ☐ Puku

Rabbit, red rock ☐ *Pronolagus sp.* ☐ Rooi klipkonyne ☐ Rothase ☐ Lièvre roux
Rat, Brant's whistling ☐ *Parotomys brantsii* ☐ Brants–fluitrot
Rat, brown ☐ *Rattus norvegicus* ☐ Bruinrot ☐ Wanderratte ☐ Rat brun/surmulot
Rat, giant ☐ *Cricetomys gambianus* ☐ Reuserot ☐ Riesen–Hamsterratte ☐ Rat de Gambie
Rat, house ☐ *Rattus rattus* ☐ Huisrot ☐ Hausratte ☐ Rat commun
Rat, Karoo bush ☐ *Otomys unisulcatus* ☐ Boskaroorot
Rat, root ☐ *Tachyoryctes splendens* ☐ Wortelrot ☐ Glanz–Schnellwühler
Rat, vlei ☐ *Otomys irroratus* ☐ Vleirot ☐ Sumpf–Lamellenzahnratte
Reedbuck, bohor ☐ *Redunca redunca* ☐ Bohor–rietbok ☐ Bohor–Riedbock ☐ Redunca
Reedbuck, mountain ☐ *Redunca fulvorufula* ☐ Rooiribbok ☐ Bergriedbock ☐ Redunca de montagne
Reedbuck, southern ☐ *Redunca arundinum* ☐ Rietbok ☐ Großriedbock ☐ Cobe des roseaux
Rhebok, grey ☐ *Pelea capreolus* ☐ Vaalribbok ☐ Rehantilope ☐ Pelea
Rhinoceros, black (hook–lipped) ☐ *Diceros bicornis* ☐ Swartrenoster ☐ Spitzmaulnashorn ☐
      Rhinocéros noir

Rhinoceros, white (square–lipped) □ *Ceratotherium simum* □ Witrenoster □ Breitmaulnashorn □
           Rhinocéros blanc
Roan □ *Hippotragus equinus* □ Bastergemsbok □ Pferdeantilope □ Hippotrague
Royal antelope □ *Neotragus pygmaeus* □ Dwergantilope □ Kleinstböckchen □ Antilope royale

Sable □ *Hippotragus niger* □ Swartwitpens □ Rappenantilope □ Hippotrague noir
Serval □ *Felis serval* □ Tierboskat □ Serval □ Serval
Sheep, domestic □ *Ovis aries* □ Skaap □ Hausschaf □ Mouton
Sitatunga □ *Tragelaphus spekei* □ Waterkoedoe □ Sitatunga □ Sitatunga
Springbok □ *Antidorcas marsupialis* □ Springbok □ Springbok □ Springbok
Springhare □ *Pedetes capensis* □ Springhaas □ Springhase □ Lièvre sauteur
Squirrel, southern ground □ *Xerus inauris* □ Waaiersterteekhoring □ Kap–Borstenhörnchen □
           Écureuil foisseur
Squirrel, tree □ *Paraxerus cepapi* □ Boomeekhoring □ Baumhörnchen □ L'Écureuils des bois
Steenbok □ *Raphicerus campestris* □ Steenbok □ Steinböckchen □ Steenbok
Suni □ *Neotragus moschatus* □ Soeni □ Suni □ Suni
Suricate □ *Suricata suricatta* □ Stokstertmeerkat □ Surikate(Erdmännchen) □ Suricate

Topi □ *Damaliscus korrigum* □ Topi □ Topi □ Topi
Tsessebe □ *Damaliscus lunatus* □ Tsessebe □ Halbmondantilope □ Sassaby

Warthog □ *Phacochoerus aethiopicus* □ Vlakvark □ Warzenschwein □ Phacochère
Waterbuck □ *Kobus ellipsiprymnus* □ Waterbok □ Ellipsenwasserbock □ Cobe à croissant
Weasel, striped □ *Poecilogale albinucha* □ Slangmuishond □ Weißnackenwiesel □ Poecilogale
Wildebeest, black □ *Connochaetes gnu* □ Swart Wildebeest □ Weißschwanzgnu □ Gnou à queue blanche
Wildebeest, blue □ *Connochaetes taurinus* □ Blouwildebees □ Streifengnu □ Gnou à queue noire
Zebra, Cape mountain/Hartmann's □ *Equus zebra* □ Kaapse bergsebra/Hartmann–bergsebra □
           Kapbergzebra/Hartmanns Bergzebra □ Zèbre de montagne
Zebra, Grevy's □ *Equus grevyi* □ Grevy–sebra □ Grevyzebra □ Zèbre de Grévy
Zebra, plains □ *Equus burchelli* □ Bontzebra □ Steppenzebra □ Zèbre de Burchell

BIRD LIST

Common English names have been used throughout the text, in this list you can find the scientific (in italics), Afrikaans, German and French names (where available) for the birds mentioned in the text.

Avocet □ *Recurvirostra avosetta* □ Bontelsie □ Säbelschnäbler □ Avocette élégante

Barbet, blackcollared □ *Lybius torquatus* □ Rooikophoutkapper □ Rotkopf–Bartvogel □ Barbican à collier
Barbet, Macclounie's □ *Lybius macclounii* □ Macclouniesehoutkapper □ Macclouniebartvogel □ Barbican de McClounie
Barbet, pied □ *Lybius leucomelas* □ Bonthoutkapper □ Rotstirnbartvogel □ Barbican pie
Bee-eater, carmine □ *Merops nubicoides* □ Rooiborsbyvreter □ Karminspint □ Guêpier écarlate
Bee–eater, European □ *Merops apiaster* □ Europese Byvreter □ Europäischer Bienenfresser □ Guêpier d'Europe
Bishop, Cape □ *Euplectes capensis* □ Kaapse Flap □ Samtwida □ L'Euplecte noir et jaune
Bishop, red □ *Euplectes oryx* □ Rooivink □ Oryxweber
Bokmakierie □ *Telophorus zeylonus* □ Bokmakierie □ Backbakiri □ Gladiateur bacbakiri
Bustard, kori □ *Ardeotis kori* □ Gompou □ Riesentrappe,Koritrappe □ Outarde kori
Bustard, Ludwig's □ *Neotis ludwigii* □ Ludwigse Pau □ Ludwigstrappe □ Outarde de Ludwig
Buzzard, augur □ *Buteo augur* □ Witborsjakkalsvoël □ Augur–Bussard □ Buse augure
Buzzard, jackal □ *Buteo rufofuscus* □ Rooiborsjakkalsvoël □ Schakalbussard □ Buse rounoir
Buzzard, steppe □ *Buteo buteo* □ Bruinjakkalsvoël □ Mäusebussard □ Buse variable

Chat, Karoo □ *Gercomela schlegelii* □ Karoospekvreter
Coot, redknobbed (crested) □ *Fulica cristata* □ Bleshoender □ Kammbleßralle □ Foulque à crête
Cormorant, Cape □ *Phalacrocorax capensis* □ Trekduiker □ Kapkormoran □ Cormoran du Cap
Cormorant, reed □ *Phalacrocorax africanus* □ Rietduiker □ Riedkormoran □ Cormoran africain
Cormorant, whitebreasted □ *Phalacrocorax carbo* □ Witborsduiker □ Weißbrustkormoran □ Grand Cormoran
Crane, blue □ *Anthropoides paradisea* □ Bloukraanvoël □ Paradieskranich □ Grue de paradis
Crane, crowned □ *Balearica regulorum* □ Mahem □ Kronenkranich □ Grue royale
Crane, wattled □ *Grus carunculata* □ Lelkraanvoël □ Klunkerkranich
Crombec, longbilled □ *Sylvietta rufescens* □ Bosveldstompstert □ Kurzschwanzsylvietta □ Fauvette crombec à long bec
Crow, black □ *Corvus capensis* □ Swartkraai □ Kapkrähe □ Corbeau du Cap
Crow, pied □ *Corvus albus* □ Witborskraai □ Schildrabe □ Corbeau pie
Cuckooo, redchested □ *Cuculus solitarius* □ Piet–my–vrou □ Einsiedlerkuckuck □ Coucou solitaire

Darter □ *Anhinga melanogaster* □ Slanghalsvoël □ Schlangenhalsvogel □ Anhinga roux
Dikkop, spotted □ *Burhinus capensis* □ Dikkop □ Kaptriel/Fleckentriel □ Edicnème tachard
Dove, Cape turtle □ *Streptopelia capicola* □ Gewone Tortelduif □ Kapturteltaube □ Tourterelle du Cap
Dove, Namaqua □ *Oena capensis* □ Namakwaduifie □ Kaptäubchen □ Tourtelette à masque de fer
Duck, yellowbilled □ *Anas undulata* □ Geelbekeend □ Gelbschnabelente □ Canard à bec jaune

Eagle, African hawk □ *Hieraaetus fasciatus* □ Afrikaanse Jagarend □ Habichtsadler □ Aigle de Bonelli
Eagle, black (Verreaux's) □ *Aquila verrauxii* □ Witkruisarend □ Verreaux–Adler □ Aigle de Verreaux
Eagle, blackbreasted snake □ *Circaetus gallicus* □ Swartborsslangarend □ Schlangenadler □ Circaète Jean–le–Blanc
Eagle, booted □ *Hieraaetus pennatus* □ Dwergarend □ Zwergadler □ Aigle botté
Eagle, crowned □ *Stephanoaetus coronatus* □ Kroonarend □ Kronenadler □ Aigle blanchard
Eagle, fish □ *Haliaaetus vocifer* □ Visarend □ Schreiseeadler □ Pygargue vocifer
Eagle, tawny □ *Aquila rapax* □ Roofarend □ Steppenadler/Raubadler □ Aigle ravisseur
Eagle, Wahlberg's □ *Aquila wahlbergi* □ Bruinarend □ Wahlbergs Adler □ Aigle de Wahlberg
Egret, cattle □ *Bubulcus ibis* □ Bosluisvoël □ Kuhreiher □ Héron garde–boeufs
Egret, little □ *Egretta garzetta* □ Kleinwitreier □ Seidenreiher □ Aigrette garzette

Falcon, lanner □ *Falco biarmicus* □ Edelvalk □ Lannerfalke □ Faucon lanier

Falcon, peregrine □ *Falco peregrinus* □ Swerfvalk □ Wanderfalke □ Faucon pèlerin

Falcon, pygmy □ *Polihierax semitorquatus* □ Dwergvalk □ Halsband–Zwergfalke □
Fauconnet d'Afrique

Falcon, rednecked □ *Falco chicquera* □ Rooinekvalk □ Rothalsfalke

Flamingo, greater □ *Phoenicopterus ruber* □ Grootflamink □ Rosa Flamingo □ Flamant rose

Flamingo, lesser □ *Phoenicopterus minor* □ Kleinflamink □ *Phoeniconaias* □ Zwergflamingo □
Petit Flamant

Flycatcher, paradise □ *Terpsiphone viridis* □ Paradysvlieëvanger □ Afrikan. Paradiesschnäpper □
Gobe–mouches paradis à longs brins

Francolin, Cape □ *Francolinus capensis* □ Kaapse Fisant □ Kapfrankolin □ Francolin criard

Francolin, crested □ *Francolinus sephaena* □ Bospatrys □ Schopffrankolin/Kappenfrankolin □
Francolin huppé

Francolin, Natal □ *Francolinus natalensis* □ Natalse Fisant □ Natalfrankolin □ Francolin du Natal

Francolin, redbilled □ *Francolinus adspersus* □ Rooibekfisant □ Rotschnabel–Frankolin □
Francolin à bec rouge

Francolin, redwinged □ *Francolinus levaillantii* □ Rooivlerkpatrys □ Rotflügelfrankolin □
Francolin de Levaillant

Francolin, Swainson's □ *Francolinus swainsonii* □ Bosveldfisant □ Swainsonfrankolin □
Francolin de Swainson

Goose, Egyptian □ *Alopochen aegyptiacus* □ Kolgans □ Nilgans □ Ouette d'Egypte

Goose, spurwing □ *Plectroperus gambensis* □ Wildemakou □ Sporengans □ Plectroptère de Gambie

Goshawk, pale chanting □ *Melierax canorus* □ Bleeksingvalk □ Singhabicht □ Autour–chanteur pâle

Grebe, little (dabchick) □ *Tachybaptus ruficollis* □ Kleindobbertjie □ Zwergtaucher □
Grèbe castagneux

Griffon, Rüppell's □ *Gyps rueppellii* □ Ruppell–Kransaasvoël □ Sperbergeier (Rüppellgeier) □
Vautour de Rüppell

Griffon (Vulture), Cape □ *Gyps coprotheres* □ Kransaasvoël □ Kapgeier □ Vautour chassefiente

Guineafowl, helmeted □ *Numida meleagris* □ Gewone Tarentaal □ Helmperlhuhn □ Pintade sauvage

Gull, kelp □ *Larus dominicanus* □ Swartrugmeeu □ Dominikanermöwe □ Goéland dominicain

Hamerkop □ *Scopus umbretta* □ Hamerkop □ Hammerkopf □ Ombrette du Sénégal

Heron, blackheaded □ *Ardea melanocephala* □ Swartkopreier □ Schwarzhalsreiher □
Héron mélanocéphale

Heron, greenbacked □ *Butorides striatus* □ Groenrugreier □ Mangrove–Reiher □ Héron vert

Heron, grey □ *Ardea cinerea* □ Bloureier □ Graureiher □ Héron cendré

Hoopoe, African □ *Upupa epops* □ Hoephoep □ Wiedehopf □ Huppe fasciée

Hoopoe, scimitarbilled wood □ *Phoeniculus cyanomelas* □ Swartbekkakelaar □ Sichelhopf □
Irrisor namaquois

Hornbill, grey □ *Tockus nasutus* □ Grysneushoringvoël □ Grautoko □ Calao nasique

Hornbill, ground □ *Bucorvus leadbeateri* □ Bromvoël □ Südlicher Hornrabe □ Calao terrestre

Hornbill, redbilled □ *Tockus erythrorhynchus* □ Rooibekneushoringvoël □ Rotschnabeltoko

Ibis, hadeda □ *Bostrychia hagedash* □ Hadeda □ Hagedash Ibis □ Ibis hagedash

Ibis, sacred □ *Threskiornis aethiopicus* □ Skoorsteenveer □ Heiliger Ibis

Ibis, southern bald □ *Geronticus calvus* □ Kalkoenibis □ Glatzenibis □ Ibis du Cap

Jacana, African □ *Actophilornis* □ Grootlangtoon □ *Actophilornis africana* □ Afrikan.Blatthühnchen □
Jacana à poitrine dorée

Kestrel, greater □ *Falco rupicoloides* □ Grootrooivalk □ Steppenfalke □ Faucon aux yeux blancs

Kestrel, lesser □ *Falco naumanni* □ Kleinrooivalk □ Rötelfalke □ Faucon crécerellette

Kestrel, rock (common) □ *Falco tinnunculus* □ Kransvalk □ Turmfalke □ Crécerelle des clochers

Kingfisher, chocolateflanked □ *Halcyon badius* □ Bruinrugvisvanger □ Braunrückenliest □
Martin–chasseur marron

Kingfisher, pied □ *Ceryle rudis* □ Bontvisvanger □ Graufischer □ Alcyon pie

Kingfisher, woodland □ *Halcyon senegalensis* □ Bosveldvisvanger □ Waldfischer □
    Martin–chasseur du Sénégal

Martin, rock □ *Hirundo fuligula* □ Kransswael □ Felsenschwalbe □ Hirondelle isabelline
Mousebird, whitebacked □ *Colius colius* □ Witkruismuisvoël □ Weißrückenmausvogel □
    Coliou à dos blanc

Nightjar, freckled □ *Caprimulgus tristigma* □ Donkernaguil □ Gefleckte Nachtschwalbe □
    Engoulevent pointillé
Nightjar, rufouscheeked □ *Caprimulgus rufigena* □ Rooiwangnaguil □ Rostwangennachtschwalbe □
    Engoulevent à joues rousses

Ostrich □ *Struthio camelus* □ Volstruis □ Strauß □ Autruche d'Afrique
Owl, barred □ *Glaucidium capense* □ Gebande uil
Owl, barn □ *Tyto alba* □ Nonnetjie–uil □ Schleiereule □ Effraie des clochers
Owl, Cape (Mackinder's) eagle □ *Bubo capensis* □ Kaapse Ooruil □ Kapuhu □ Grand–Duc du Cap
Owl, giant eagle □ *Bubo lacteus* □ Reuse Ooruil □ Milchuhu □ Grand–Duc de Verreaux
Owl, grass □ *Tyto capensis* □ Grasuil □ Graseule □ Effraie du Cap
Owl, pearlspotted □ *Glaucidium perlatum* □ Witkoluil □ Perlkauz □ Chevêchette perlée
Owl, scops □ *Otus senegalensis* □ skopsuil □ Zwergohreule
Owl, spotted eagle □ *Bubo africanus* □ Gevlekte Ooruil □ Fleckenuhu □ Grand–Duc africain
Owl, whitefaced □ *Otus leucotis* □ Witwanguil □ Weißgesichtohreule □ Petit–Duc à face blanche
Owl, wood □ *Stix woodfordii* □ Bosuil

Parrot, Rüppell's □ *Poicephalus rueppellii* □ Bloupenspapegaai □ Rüppellpapagei □
      Perroquet de Rüppell
Pelican, white □ *Pelecanus onocrotalus* □ Witpelikaan □ Rosapelikan □ Pélican blanc
Pigeon, rock (speckled) □ *Columba guinea* □ Kransduif □ Guineataube □ Pigeon roussard
Plover, blacksmith □ *Vanellus armatus* □ Bontekiewiet □ Waffenkiebitz
Plover, crowned □ *Vanellus coronatus* □ Kroonkiewiet □ Kronenkiebitz □ Vanneau couronné
Plover, threebanded □ *Charadrius tricollaris* □ Driebandstrandkiewiet □ Dreibandregenpfeifer □
      Pluvier à triple collier
Plover, whitefronted □ *Charadrius marginatus* □ Vaalstrandkiewiet □ Weißstirnregenpfeifer □
      Pluvier à front blanc
Pochard, redeyed (southern) □ *Netta erythrophthalma* □ Bruineend □ Rotaugenente □ Nette brune
Prinia, spotted □ *Prinia maculosa* □ Karoolangstertjie □ Gefleckte Prinia □ Prinia tachetée

Quelea, redbilled □ *Quelea quelea* □ Rooibekkwelea □ Blutschnabelweber □ Travailleur à bec rouge

Raven, whitenecked □ *Corvus albicollis* □ Withalskraai □ Geierrabe □ Corbeau à cou blanc
Robin, Heuglin's □ *Cossypha heuglini* □ Heuglinse Janfrederik □ Heuglinrötel □ Cossyphe de Heuglin
Roller, lilacbreasted □ *Coracias caudata* □ Gewone Troupant □ Gabelracke □ Rollier à longs brins

Sandgrouse, blackfaced □ *Pterocles decorathus* □ Sandpatrys □ Flughuhn
Sandgrouse, Namaqua □ *Pterocles namaqua* □ Kelkiewyn □ Namakwaflughuhn □ Ganga namaqua
Sandpiper, curlew □ *Calidris ferruginea* □ Krombekstrandloper □ Sichelstrandläufer □ Bécasseau cocorli
Secretarybird □ *Sagittarius serpentarius* □ Sekretarisvoël □ Sekretär □ Messager serpentaire
Shelduck □ *Tadorna cana* □ Kopereend □ Graukopfkasarka □ Tadorne à tête grise
Shrike, fiscal □ *Lanius collaris* □ Fiskaallaksman □ Fiskalwürger □ Pie–grièche fiscale
Sparrow, Cape □ *Passer melanurus* □ Gewone Mossie □ Kapsperling □ Moineau mélanure
Sparrow, great □ *Passer motitensis* □ Grootmossie □ Rotbrauner Sperling □ Moineau roux
Sparrow, house □ *Passer domesticus* □ Huismossie □ Haussperling □ Moineau domestique
Sparrowhawk, little □ *Accipiter minullus* □ Kleinsperwer □ Zwergsperber □ Epervier minulle
Starling, glossy □ *Lamprotornis nitens* □ Kleinglansspreeu □ Rotschulterglanzstar □
      Merle à épaulettes rouges
Starling, pied □ *Spreo bicolor* □ Witgatspreeu □ Zweifarbenglanzstar □ Spréo
Starling, redwinged □ *Onychognathus morio* □ Rooivlerkspreeu □ Rotschwingenstar □ Roupenne

Starling, wattled □ *Creatophora cinerea* □ Lelspreeu □ Lappenstar
Stilt, blackwinged □ *Himantopus himantopus* □ Rooipootelsie □ Stelzenläufer □ Echasse blanche
Stork, black □ *Ciconia nigra* □ Grootswartooievaar □ Schwarzstorch □ Cigogne noir
Stork, marabou □ *Leptoptilos crumeniferus* □ Maraboe □ Afrikanischer Marabu □ Marabout d'Afrique
Stork, saddlebilled □ *Ephippiorhynchus senegalensis* □ Saalbekooievaar □ Sattelstorch □
       Jabiru du Sénégal
Stork, white □ *Ciconia ciconia* □ Witooievaar □ Weißer Storch □ Cigogne blanche
Stork, yellowbilled □ *Mycteria ibis* □ Nimmersat □ Nimmersatt □ Tantale ibis
Sunbird, malachite □ *Nectarinia formosa* □ Jangroentjie □ Malachitnektarvogel □
       Soui–manga (nectarin) malachite
Sunbird, Neergard's □ *Nectarinia neergaardi* □ Bloukruissuikerbekkie □ Neergaardnektarvogel □
       Nectarin de Neergard
Swallow, greaterstriped □ *Hirundo cucullata* □ Grootstreepswael □ Streifenschwalbe □
       Hirondelle à tête rousse
Swallow, lesserstriped □ *Hirundo abyssinica* □ Kleinstreepswael □ Kleine Streifenschwalbe □
       Hirondelle striée
Swallow, mosque □ *Hirundo senegalensis* □ Moskeeswael □ Moscheeschwalbe □
       Hirondelle des mosquées
Swallow, pearlbreasted □ *Hirundo dimidiata* □ Perelborsswael □ Perlbrustschwalbe
Swallow, redbreasted □ *Hirundo semirufa* □ Rooiborsswael □ Rotbauchschwalbe □
       Hirondelle à ventre roux
Swallow, South African cliff □ *Hirundo spilodera* □ Familieswael □ Klippenschwalbe □
       Hirondelle sud–africaine
Swallow, whitethroated □ *Hirundo albigularis* □ Witkeelswael
Swallow, wiretailed □ *Hirundo smithii* □ Draadstertswael

Tern, whiskered □ *Chlidonias hybridas* □ Witbaardsterretjie □ Weißbartseeschwalbe □ Guifette moustac
Thrush, olive □ *Turdus olivaceus* □ Olyflyster □ Rotbauchdrossel □ Grive olivâtre
Tit, Cape penduline □ *Anthoscopus minutus* □ Kaapse Kapokvoël □ Kapbeutelmeise □ Rémiz du Cap
Trogan, narina □ *Apalodema narina* □ Bosberrie □ Narina trogan
Turaco, Knysna □ *Tauraco corythaix* □ Knysnaloerie □ Federhelmturako □ Touraco louri
Turaco (lourie), purplecrested □ *Tauraco porphyreolophus* □ Bloukuifloerie □ Glanzhaubenturako □
       Touraco à huppe splendide

Vulture, hooded □ *Necrosyrtes monachus* □ Monnikaasvoël □ Kappengeier □ Vautour charognard
Vulture, lappetfaced □ *Torgos tracheliotus* □ Swartaasvoël □ Ohrengeier □ Vautour oricou
Vulture, whitebacked □ *Gyps africanus* □ Witrugaasvoël □ Weißrückengeier/Zwerggänsegeier □
       Vautour africain

Wagtail, Cape □ *Motacilla capensis* □ Gewone Kwikkie □ Kapstelze □ Bergeronette du Cap
Warbler, rufouseared □ *Malcorus pectoralis* □ Rooioorlangstertjie □ Rotohrensänger
Weaver, blackcapped social □ *Pseudonigrita cabanisi* □ Swartkop–versamelvoël □
       Schwarzkopf–Siedelweber
Weaver, brownthroated □ *Ploceus xanthopterus* □ Bruinkeelwewer □ Braunkchlweber □
       Tisseriu à gorge brune
Weaver, Cape □ *Ploceus capensis* □ Kaapse Wewer □ Kapweber □ Tisserin du Cap
Weaver, chestnut □ *Ploceus rubuginosus* □ Bruinwewer □ Rotbrauner Weber
Weaver, forest □ *Ploceus bicolor* □ Bosmusikant □ Waldweber □ Tisserin bicolore
Weaver, golden □ *Ploceus xanthops* □ Goudwewer □ Goldweber □ Tisserin doré
Weaver, lessermasked □ *Ploceus intermedius* □ Kleingeelvink □ Cabanisweber □
       Tisserin masqué d'Afrique du Sud
Weaver, masked □ *Ploceus velatus* □ Swartkeelgeelvink □ Maskenweber □
       Tisserin masquée d'Afrique occidentale
Weaver, redbilled buffalo □ *Bubalornis niger* □ Buffelwewer □ Rotschnabel–Büffelweber □
Weaver, redheaded □ *Anaplectes rubriceps* □ Rooikopwewer □ Rotkopfweber □
       Tisserin–malimbe écarlate
Weaver, sociable □ *Philetairus socius* □ Versamelvoël □ Siedelweber □ Tisserin social

Weaver, spectacled □ *Ploceus ocularis* □ Brilwewer □ Brillenweber □ Tisserin à lunettes oriental

Weaver, spottedbacked □ *Ploceus cucullatus* □ Bontrugwewer □ Dorfweber □ Tisserin des villages

Weaver, thickbilled □ *Amblyospiza albifrons* □ Dikbekwewer □ Weißstirnweber □ Tisserin à front blanc

Weaver, whitebrowed sparrow □ *Plocepasser mahali* □ Koringvoël □ Mahaliweber □ Mahali

Weaver, yellow □ *Ploceus subaureus* □ Geelwewer □ Goldweber

Woodpecker, bearded □ *Thripias namaquus* □ Baardspeg □ Bartspecht □ Pic barbu

Woodpecker, buffspotted □ *Campethera nivosa* □ Bruingevlektespeg □ Pic tacheté

Woodpecker, cardinal □ *Dendropicos fuscescens* □ Kardinaalspeg □ Kardinalspecht □ Pic cardinal

Woodpecker, goldentailed □ *Campethera abingoni* □ Goudstertspeg □ Goldschwanzspecht □
    Pic à queue dorée

Woodpecker, ground □ *Geocolaptes olivaceus* □ Grondspeg □ Bodenspecht □ Pic laboureur

INDEX

302